Internet Users' Guide to Network Resource Tools

Internet Users' Guide to Network Resource Tools

Written for the Trans-European Research and Education Networking Association (TERENA)

by

Margaret Isaacs

Addison-Wesley

Harlow, England • Reading, Massachusetts • Menlo Park, California
New York • Don Mills, Ontario • Amsterdam • Bonn • Sydney • Singapore
Tokyo • Madrid • San Juan • Milan • Mexico City • Seoul • Taipei

Published by
Addison Wesley Longman Limited
Edinburgh Gate
Harlow
Essex CM20 2JE
England

and Associated Companies throughout the World.

Acknowledgements for reproduction of copyright material appear following the trademark notice on page xi.

Cover designed by Senate
Typeset in 9.5/12pt StoneSerif by 43
Printed and bound in Great Britain by Henry Ling Ltd,
at the Dorset Press, Dorchester, Dorset

First printed 1998

ISBN 0-201-36055-1

British Library Cataloguing-in-Publication Data
A catalogue record for this book is available from the British Library

Contents

Preface

The original *Guide to Network Resource Tools* was produced by staff of the then European Academic and Research Network (EARN). Printed as a booklet and registered in the Internet Engineering Task Force's FYI series as RFC1580/FYI23, it became a very popular guide to using the Internet for end-users and support staff. In 1996 an update of the guide was started by EARN's successor, the Trans-European Research and Education Networking Association (TERENA), which resulted in the *Internet Users' Guide to Network Resource Tools*; this completely new version covers a wide range of popular tasks and tools on the Internet today.

The *Internet Users' Guide to Network Resource Tools* caters for a range of information requirements:

- Chapter 1, User Overview, is structured around **common user tasks** such as finding someone's email address, exchanging files with colleagues, locating companies or searching for information on a subject. Readers with a task to carry out can find suggestions on how to approach the task, information on relevant online resources and references to tools which might be used.
- Chapters 2 to 7 provide information in greater depth for users and user support staff on **tools** for a range of general network activities such as browsing, searching, group communication, providing information, and so on.
- The Index to the book also gives multiple routes of entry to the information: readers can look up a particular **task** they want to carry out (eg email addresses, finding), categories of **general information or tools** (eg security; meta-search services), or particular **named products**, services, features etc of the Internet (eg AltaVista; Internet Explorer; HTML; and so on).

The material in this book is derived from version 5.0 of the online TERENA Guide to Network Resource Tools (see Plate 1), available via `http://www.terena.nl/gnrt/`. TERENA hopes to keep this guide up to date; please mail your comments, suggestions and corrections to `gnrt@terena.nl`.

Acknowledgements

This edition is the result of a project of the TERENA TOOLDOC task force. The principal author is Margaret Isaacs (magnet@magnet-it.co.uk). Peter Valkenburg of TERENA is responsible for the technical support and project development.

The members of the review panel of the guide were Dave Hartland (Newcastle University/NetSkills), Ben Geerlings (SURFnet), Jean Ritchie (Edinburgh University), Peter Stone (NISS), Shirley Wood (UKERNA) and John Martin (TERENA). Additional support was provided by TERENA's John Dyer, Kevin Meynell and Paul Rendek.

Trademark notice

The following designations are trademarks or registered trademarks of the organizations whose names follow in brackets: Adobe Acrobat, Adobe PageMill, Photoshop (Adobe Systems Inc.); LiveAgent (AgentSoft); Allaire Forums (Allaire); Bargain Finder (Anderson Consulting); Apple VideoPhone, Macintosh, QuickTime (Apple Computer Inc.); Autonomy Agentware (Autonomy Corporation); BBEdit (Bare Bones Software); AltaVista, the AltaVista logo, the Digital logo, VMS (Digital Equipment Corporation); Intelligent Concept Extraction, OpenText (Excite); HP-UX (Hewlett Packard Company); Infoseek (a service mark of Infoseek Corporation); Communique (InSoft); Edition, ProShare (Intel Corporation); AIX, OS/2 (International Business Machines Corporation); LISTSERV (L-Soft International); Lotus Domino, Lotus Notes (Lotus Development Corporation); Lycos (Lycos, Inc.); Internet Explorer, Jscript, MS-DOS, NetMeeting, VBScript, Windows, Word (Microsoft Corporation); ICQ (Mirabilis); CoolTalk, Netscape, Netscape Communicator, Netscape Navigator, and Netscape logos (Netscape Communications Corporation); NeXT (NeXT Computer, Inc.); PGP (Pretty Good Privacy, Inc.); WebCompass (Quarterdeck Corporation); HotDog Pro (Sausage Software); HoTMetaL PRO (SoftQuad); Community Place (Sony); SPARC, SPARCstation (Sparc International Inc.); HotJava, Java, Solaris (Sun Microsystems Inc.); Search'97 (Verity); CUSeeMe (White Pine Software); Unix (licensed through X/Open Company Ltd.).

Publishers' acknowledgements

The publishers are grateful to the following for permission to reproduce copyright material. In Plate 5 screenshots from Netscape Conference, in Plates 1, 2 and 3 Netscape Browser frame, used with permission, copyright 1998 Netscape Communications Corporation, all rights reserved; the plates may not be reprinted or copied without the express written permission of Netscape; Netscape Communications Corporation has not authorized, sponsored, endorsed or approved this publication and is not responsible for its content. In Plate 2 screenshots from AltaVista reproduced with the permission of Digital Equipment Corporation. In Plate 6 screenshots of Adobe Pagemill HTML editor copyright Adobe Systems Incorporated. For Plate 3, thanks to the Social Science Information Gateway at the University of Bristol. For Plate 4, thanks to COVISE at the University of Stuttgart and the teams at INRIA and UCL. For Plate 8, thanks to Pretty Good Privacy, Inc.; screenshot reproduced by permission also from Microsoft Corporation.

1 User Overview

In Chapter 1 we look at some of the most commonly occurring information needs and suggest ways in which they might be satisfied using available network tools and services. The information needs come within the scope of the following topics:

- searching for information on a subject,
- searching for people,
- searching for companies and organizations,
- finding and retrieving software,
- communicating,
- collaborating,
- exchanging files,
- World Wide Web publishing,
- keeping up to date,
- self-protection,
- Netiquette (network etiquette).

1.1 Searching for information on a subject

Searching for information on a particular subject is one of the most common tasks undertaken by network users. There is an enormous amount of information on the networks on a vast range of subjects. It can be found on the World Wide Web, in Usenet News postings, mailing list archives, gopher menus, ftp archives and a number of other sources. Fortunately, there are now many aids to locating subject material. Some of the main ones include:

- services which automatically gather information on network resources and offer searching of the databases they generate (search engines);
- human-compiled lists of resources organized by subject (classified directories);
- quality-controlled classified lists of resources selected (and described) by a subject expert (subject gateways);
- programs which gather information personalized to your requirements (agents);

- specialist databases;
- additional Internet sources.

We shall now look at some of the strategies that can be adopted:

A first approach could be to use a WWW (World Wide Web) search engine to do a keyword search on specific terms. You can browse through the list of hits, look at the promising ones and, if necessary, follow up with refinement or rerunning the search. Web search engines yield fast results and plenty of them, usually ranked according to relevance. Their databases of Web documents and other Internet resources are vast. Many of them enable advanced searching and use complex algorithms to assess the relevance of documents. Where the full text of documents is indexed, the search engine can find a term anywhere in a document which may be useful for tracking down very specific or obscure bits of information. The main problem with search engines is that they can generate overwhelmingly large hit lists.

Some examples of search engines are:

- **AltaVista** `http://www.altavista.digital.com/` Fast and powerful full-text searcher of the WWW and News offering flexible search options;
- **Lycos** `http://www.lycos.com/` Simple and advanced searching of the WWW, gopher and ftp. Complementary classified directory;
- **Infoseek** `http://www.infoseek.com/` Searches the WWW, News and other sources; offers high-power searcher (Ultraseek) and searching/browsing interface (Ultrasmart);
- **Excite** `http://www.excite.com/` Full-text Web and News searcher designed for natural language searching. Offers concept and keyword searching with relevance feedback;
- **Euroferret** `http://www.muscat.co.uk/chd/eurotxt.htm` European search of the Web in French, German, Italian, Spanish and Swedish.

Note that many search engines provide complementary subject-organized listings.

See 'Web search engines' (Section 3.1) for further discussion and examples.

Secondly, you could work through a subject-organized (classified) directory to get to the required topic, then browse the available offerings. Classified directories offer a number of broad subject divisions at the top level, and within each of these there will be further subject subdivisions from which to choose. You can work down through the hierarchy, starting with a broad subject heading, and arriving at the specific topic of your interest, where you can look through resources dealing with that topic. Directories offer the benefit of grouping like with like, enabling you to see individual resources in their broader subject context. And because the resources are human-selected, there is probably a better chance of locating quality information than with a search engine. Classified directories usually provide a search facility on their database as well so you are not limited to browsing. Some may also provide a description and/or an evaluation of each resource.

Some examples of classified directories include:

- **Yahoo** http://www.yahoo.com/;
- **World-Wide Web Virtual Library** http://www.w3.org/hypertext/DataSources/bySubject/Overview.html;
- **Magellan** http://www.mckinley.com/ Provides descriptive entries and ratings of sites.

European directories include:

- **UK Directory** http://www.ukdirectory.com/ Subject listings of sites;
- **Index of Swedish WWW Pages** http://www.sunet.se/sweden/main.html.

See 'Subject directories' (Section 3.3) for further discussion and examples.

A third strategy could be to refer to quality controlled listings to find the best resources in a subject. Such listings attempt to distil from the mass of available resources the quality items. Commonly they will provide descriptive evaluative entries on each resource included. The scope of these listings may be general or specific to one subject area. In the latter case they are referred to as **subject gateways**. They may be free or subscription based. Their coverage of resources is obviously much smaller than robot-generated databases, but the guarantee of quality may more than compensate for this.

Some examples are:

- **InfoMine Scholarly Academic Resource Collections** http://lib-www.ucr.edu/ Classified descriptive listing of useful Internet/Web resources including databases, electronic publications, mailing lists, library catalogues and so on;
- **OMNI (Organizing Medical Networked Information)** http://www.omni.ac.uk/ Gateway to quality online medical resources, classified and catalogued;
- **NetFirst** http://www.oclc.org/oclc/netfirst/netfirst.htm Example of subscription-based service which selects, catalogues, classifies and monitors Internet resources.

See the further discussion of subject gateways in Section 3.3.2.

There is a great deal of information on the Internet but it can still be difficult to find what you seek. Search engines and directories may not filter out the extraneous low-grade material. There may not be any quality-controlled listings which focus on your subject interest. One solution is a tool which is likely to become more common in future, that is, the **intelligent agent** (Section 3.6). Agent software can be used to carry out searching on your behalf in any way you instruct it. For instance an agent might conduct regular searches of specified databases for a subject, then filter, categorize and deliver the information to you. Agents may be available on servers, or agent software may be installed on your local machine, possibly as a plug-in to a Web browser.

Examples of intelligent agents include:

- **Surfbot** `http://www.surflogic.com/` Fetches, filters and organizes WWW content;
- **Search'97** from Verity `http://www.verity.com/`.

See further references at BotSpot `http://www.botspot.com/`.

Some of the most valuable resources accessible via the Internet are the many specialist databases used as everyday working tools by librarians, scientists, and other professionals. For instance online bibliographic databases are the stock in trade of librarians, and scientific datasets figure prominently in many scientific disciplines. The databases don't necessarily comprise Web documents but may be accessed through a Web gateway which passes requests to the database engine and returns results to the user. Many, though not all, are subscription or fee-based and are accessed with a user-id and password.

Examples include:

- **Carl Uncover** `http://www.carl.org/uncover/` Periodicals database;
- **Physics E-print Archive** `http://babbage.sissa.it/` Pre-prints of physics journal articles.

There are also commercial services which seek to offer added-value searching to users by combining in one searchable database information from a range of public and proprietary sources, for example

- **NlightN** `http://www.nlightn.com/` Fee-based access to index of the WWW, news wires, reference sources and bibliographic and full text databases.

Finally, other Internet source material such as mailing lists, gopher servers, and ftp archives may contain useful subject information which slips through the mainstream net of search engines and classified directories. It is useful to know about search facilities for these specific areas of the Internet, for example

- **mailing lists** There are a number of search facilities for mailing lists and mailing list archives. See Section 1.2.1;
- **gopher servers** `gopher://veronica.scs.unr.edu/11/veronica/` Veronica is an index searcher of gopher menus. You can usually select veronica from a gopher menu;
- **ftp archives** `http://src.doc.ic.ac.uk/archie/archie.html` Archie is an index searcher of ftp archives.

1.2 Searching for people

If you plot a five-year graph of the estimated number of people using the Internet, what you will see is a soaring curve steadily reaching more and more of the world's population. Currently there are tens of millions of Internet users which, by any standards, makes the Internet an impressive people resource. Here, almost certainly, there will be people who share your interests, no matter how specialized, esoteric or eccentric. Additionally, the Internet and the many networks embraced by it provide excellent media for bringing like-minded people together and enabling them to exchange information and opinions easily.

In another quite different way, networks facilitate communication between people. They may be able to help you locate address information in order to make contact with a specific person. Sections 1.2.3 to 1.2.5 below look at the many sources to consult for information on email addresses and other contact details.

1.2.1 Locating people with common interests

Computer networks offer not only great technical and information resources, they also provide a uniquely effective vehicle for making contact with people who share common interests. They are effective because they provide a fast and efficient means of transmission, and also because they carry tens of thousands of ongoing discussion lists and newsgroups. These give groups of people with a common interest the opportunity for easy exchange of ideas and news on their subject of interest, and may also generate further one-to-one dialogues between like-minded individuals. Networks facilitate the existence of virtual communities united by common interests, irrespective of location, institutional rank, or even social skills.

To find others who share your interest in a particular subject, the most useful starting point is to identify mailing lists (discussion lists) or newsgroups which cover the topic. Use one of the services which offer searching by topic such as the following.

Mailing lists and newsgroups

- **Liszt** `http://www.liszt.com/` Large directory of mailing lists covering lists managed by LISTSERV, Listproc, Majordomo and Mailbase amongst others. Also information on thousands of newsgroups. Weekly updating of the database;
- **Tile.Net** `http://tile.net/` Searching/browsing of discussion lists and newsgroups.

Mailing lists

- **CataList: the Catalog of LISTSERV lists** `http://www.lsoft.com/lists/listref.html` Large constantly maintained catalogue of LISTSERV lists offering searching for mailing lists of interest, and browsing of public LISTSERV lists;
- **Stephanie daSilva's Publicly Accessible Mailing Lists** `http://www.neosoft.com:80/internet/paml/` List of mailing lists available primarily through the Internet and the UUCP (Unix to Unix Copy Program) network. No search facility but an alphabetical list of subjects which link to information on relevant mailing list;
- **Directory of Scholarly and Professional E-Conferences, by Diane K. Kovacs** `http://www.n2h2.com/KOVACS` Includes discussion lists, Internet interest groups, Usenet newsgroups, forums, text-based virtual reality systems such as MUDS, MOO'S, and so on. Informative entries including access instructions are provided;
- **Search the List of Lists** `http://catalog.com/vivian/interest-group-search.html` The *List of Lists* was the pioneer 'master list' of email discussion groups;
- **Mailbase** `http://www.mailbase.ac.uk/` UK-based mailing list service which administers a large number of lists primarily for the UK academic and research community. Membership of public lists is open to anyone. Use its search facility (linked to from the home page) to search for lists on serious academic or research topics.

Newsgroups

- **Usenet Info Center Launch Pad** `http://sunsite.unc.edu/usenet-b/home.html`;
- **DejaNews** `http://www.dejanews.com/` Offers keyword searching for newsgroups and also searching for newsgroup articles.

1.2.2 Finding contact details for people

On the net it is possible to locate email addresses, postal addresses, telephone numbers and even fax numbers, using searchable online directory services. What is not possible is to give any guarantees about what might or might not be able to be found. There is no universal directory of net users, nor even comprehensive coverage of names within any one country. And coverage is certainly unequal from country to country and from discipline to discipline. On the plus side, the existing directories contain millions of names and corresponding contact details. There are telephone directories, directories of fax numbers and databases of email addresses. Less obvious but also useful are directories of professional groups, databases of subscribers to mailing lists, campus and organizational directories, and a directory of people who have posted articles to Usenet newsgroups. Almost universally, these services are available via the World Wide Web. Commonly the Web is used as a gateway to an external database of names, enabling the user to query the database by simply typing search terms into a window on the Web page.

The information contained in the directories on the net may be generated by a robot which collects data from Web sites. It may be extracted from Usenet postings, submitted by Internet Service Providers (ISPs), and/or a range of manually collected sources such as organizational staff listings, or self-submitted details from users. Internet directory services may use a variety of technologies. The service may be a database held in a single location and interrogated from a single point using some sort of index searcher, or it may be a distributed database accessed through the use of a common protocol such as X.500. Information on popular tools for building and accessing directory services (such as X.500) can be found in Section 3.4.

We will now look at a few familiar requirements for contact details for people and suggest various approaches.

1.2.3 Finding email addresses

One of the most common requirements for network users wanting to correspond with others is for information on email addresses. Here are some suggestions for finding the email address of a would-be correspondent:

(1) Ask them! (Use the phone if necessary.)
(2) Ask them to email you first, then use your email program's Reply function. This generates their email address in the 'To:' field of the message. Make a note of it for future reference, or better still, get your email program to make a note of it for you. Most email programs will have such a facility, entitled 'Nicknames', 'Aliases', or something similar.
(3) Search an online directory service. Here are some which have substantial databases of names:

   - **Four11** `http://www.four11.com/` More than 7 million unique email addresses;
   - **Whowhere** `http://www.whowhere.com/` Online White Pages service comprising several databases including email addresses, US phone numbers and postal addresses, home pages, Internet Phone directory, company Web sites, and others;
   - **Internet Address Finder** `http://www.iaf.net/` Searching by personal name or domain name. Available in English, Dutch, French, German, Italian and Portuguese;
   - **Bigfoot** `http://www.bigfoot.com/` If a search is unsuccessful, Bigfoot will provide a list of suggestions. Also offers tips on searching. Available in English, French, German, Italian, Japanese and Spanish;

- **World Email Directory** http://worldemail.com/ Provides access to millions of email, business and phone addresses worldwide. Uses WebCrawler to collect data and provides a powerful search engine with flexible search capability;
- **X.500 directory services** X.500 is a standard for directory services enabling a user with an X.500 client to access the global net of X.500 directory services via any X.500 server. You can search for a person's contact details within an organization, a country, or if you have no information to start with, conduct a global search. X.500 directories of staff details are maintained by many organizations throughout the world and national directories are available in many countries such as Austria, Belgium, Denmark, Germany, Hungary, Italy, Luxembourg, the Netherlands, Norway, Poland, Slovakia, Slovenia, Spain, Sweden, Switzerland, the UK and the USA.

  See this page from Dante for details: http://www.dante.net/np/pdi.html. A UK Web Gateway, the Worldwide Directory Service, is at: http://www.cse.bris.ac.uk/comms/ccrjh/search-form-world.html. In the US, the Internic also provides a country listing for X.500 searching: http://ds1.internic.net:8888/.

(4) Databases of mailing list subscribers and Usenet news contributors are another useful source for email addresses, particularly if your correspondent is an Internet enthusiast and likely to participate in online discussions. These are ones to try:

- **Usenet addresses directory** http://usenet-addresses.mit.edu/ Database amassed from addresses of people who have posted to Usenet newsgroups over the period 1991 to 1996. Links to local directory services facilitate verification of the address;
- **AltaVista** http://www.altavista.digital.com/ AltaVista's database includes Usenet postings, including the name and email address of contributors. This provides a supplementary update to the data in the Usenet addresses directory. To use, select Usenet rather than Web as the search option, type in the name of the person in the search window, then press Return;
- **Mailbase** http://www.mailbase.ac.uk/ Searchable database of subscribers. Mailbase administers some hundreds of mailing lists and its database of names, mainly from the academic and research community, is substantial. Though the service is UK based, the subscriber base is international. Under Searching Facilities, select Look for an Email Address.

(5) Organizational directory listings
If your would-be correspondent is at a university or research institute, the institution's staff list may provide the information you need. Institutional Web sites (Web search services may be useful in locating

particular ones) will commonly provide a link to a searchable directory listing of personnel. Many organizations use a directory service called CSO (sometimes referred to as Phonebook) to make contact details available (see Section 3.4.1). The Phonebook Gateway–Server Lookup at `http://www.uiuc.edu/cgi-bin/ph/lookup` provides links to hundreds of organizations' CSO servers all over the world.

Companies are less likely to make their staff lists available publicly, though some are online.

(6) Professional listings provide another possible source of contact details. Web search services may be useful for locating the Web sites of professional associations. For example, use a search engine to search for:

```
professional association accountants Ireland
```

Also accessible through the Web are discipline-based personnel listings, such as the HEP (High Energy Physics) E-mail Database at `http://www.slac.stanford.edu/spires/form/hepnspif.html`.

References

FAQ: How to find people's E-mail addresses
`http://www.qucis.queensu.ca/FAQs/email/finding.html`

1.2.4 Finding telephone numbers and postal addresses

USA

The USA has data from multiple telephone directories on the Internet.

- **555-1212.com Web site** `http://www.555-1212.com/` Offers searching of a number of telephone databases. These same databases of US numbers are available elsewhere as well, such as from Yahoo, Four11, Switchboard and other services;
- Another substantial US source is **Infospace's people search** at `http://in-101.infospace.com/iui/people.htm`.

Other countries

Searchable telephone directories for a number of other countries are also available. Currently these include Argentina, Australia, Belgium, Canada, France, Malaysia, the Netherlands, New Zealand, Singapore and Slovenia.

- **555-1212.com Web site** `http://www.555-1212/white_all.htm` Provides links to each country's White Pages service;

- **Global Yellow Pages** http://www.globalyp.com/world.htm Provides links to national residential telephone and business directories.

Internal phone directories

Though internal phone directories are a valuable source of information on individual contact details, only a proportion are available on the net and few are publicized, perhaps discouraged by data protection laws. One route to locating the directories of individual institutions or companies is to use a WWW search engine to search for the organization name, or just take a guess at the domain name, for example 'www.company-name.com' and point your browser to it. There is however, a ready-made (though selective) list called *Telephone Directories on the Net* at http://www.procd.com/hl/direct.htm. This includes businesses, goverment and educational institutions worldwide.

1.2.5 Finding fax numbers

These are some sources to search for fax numbers:

- **Kapitol Listing of International Directories** http://www.infobel.be/infobel/infobelworld.html Links to World Telecom Fax directory searching for many countries from here, plus links to some Yellow Pages;
- **555-1212.com Web site** http://www.555-1212.com/fax_all.htm Country listings of fax directories;
- **Global Yellow Pages** http://www.globalyp.com/world.htm Mixed directory listing;
- **InfoSpace – World listing** http://in-101.infospace.com/iui/intl/int.html List of world directories by region. Covers White Pages, Yellow Pages and fax directories;
- **InfoSpace – USA and Canada** http://in-101.infospace.com/iui/fax.html Search for fax numbers in the USA and Canada.

1.3 Searching for companies and organizations

There are a number of approaches to searching for companies and organizations on the net. Many companies and organizations now have their own Web pages, so Web search services are a good starting point. There are also directories and databases not directly indexed by search engines. The following approaches may be useful:

- conduct a keyword search of search engine database (use as many terms as possible, for example organization name, type of organization, product, location);

- (crude but effective) guess the URL of a Web page, for example http://www.companyname.com/ or http://www.organizationname.org/ or http://www.organizationname.org.countrycode/;
- use the online email, telephone and fax directories mentioned in Sections 1.2.3 to 1.2.5;
- consult the relevant directories, for example
  - **World Wide Yellow Pages** http://www.yellow.com/ Searching or browsing for companies worldwide;
  - **WhoWhere?: Companies on the Net** http://www.whowhere.com/ Extensive world wide directory of company whereabouts on the net;
  - **EuroBusiness Centre** http://www.euromktg.com/euromktg/eurobus.html;
  - **YellowWeb Europe** http://www.yweb.com/ Multilingual;
  - **BigYellow** http://s18.bigyellow.com/ Search or browse by topic for US businesses. Includes listings of European Yellow Pages at http://s18.bigyellow.com/global/Europe.html;
  - **A Business Compass** http://www.abcompass.com/ Keyword search or browsable listings by subject, industry or geography. (Limited number of European sites.) Detailed entries on companies included.
- check world wide fax and telephone directories http://worldemail.com/wede4ab.shtml;
- consult professional directories, for example
  - **Worldwide Banking Directory** http://www.orcc.com/banks.htm;
  - **HEP Virtual Phonebook** http://www.hep.net/sites/directories.html Links to phonebooks and directories of High Energy Physics sites or experiments around the world. Also links to email and White Pages databases for high energy physicists;
  - **Martindale-Hubbell Lawyer Locator** http://www.martindale.com/locator/home.html Searching on a database of 900 000 lawyers and law firms around the world.

1.4 Finding and retrieving software

Computer networks are great treasure troves of computer software. Public archives on the Internet and other networks contain millions of public domain software and shareware packages which are easily accessed and downloaded. An ethos of free exchange and sharing, a climate of experimentation and development, and a potent concentration of computing talent has generated these enormous quantities of good working software available at little or no cost, with developers enjoying the benefits of network distribution, testing and feedback. Much of the software is in the public domain and free; there is also a good deal of shareware. Shareware requires payment to the author, but even here there is usually a free trial period allowed. The Internet also provides access to software from commercial software companies such as Microsoft, Adobe and others. Some is available free, such as Microsoft Internet Explorer or Adobe Acrobat Reader, but online ordering and purchase of commercial software is also viable. For online purchase using a credit card, there are protective security mechanisms such as Secure Sockets Layer (SSL) employed in the communication between browser and server. For those who are uneasy about sending their encrypted credit card details off on the Internet, the vendors usually provide alternative routes for payment. For more information on security see Chapter 6.

Knowing that there is a lot of software available is cheering, but browsing through cryptically signposted ftp archives is a very frustrating exercise. For effective use of ftp resources, it's advisable to be aware of a few useful tools and services. Some suggestions follow.

Make use of WWW software directories

When you come to look for a software package, some of the large well-organized WWW software directories are a useful starting point (see Section 1.4.1). They classify each item within a broad category making it possible to browse purposefully, whether or not you can put a name to the software you need. They also offer searching. If you know what you want the software to do then you should be able to search for it. For instance, you could search for a paint program using the search term `paint`, or an ftp client with the search term `ftp`. And you would be able to specify the operating system for which it is required.

Familiarize yourself with ftp

Files are transferred from one Internet computer to another using a protocol called **ftp** (File Transfer Protocol). Basically, this is just an agreed set of commands used between ftp clients and servers. Ftp is used in downloading files from ftp archives, or uploading files to your own directory on a remote server. For more information on ftp see Chapter 7.

Anonymous ftp

There is a very useful enhancement of ftp called **anonymous ftp**. This is a convention which effectively provides open access to software in public ftp archives. There are basically two routes for using anonymous ftp:

(1) **ftp connection using an ftp client** When prompted for a login, type in `anonymous`, then give your email address as the password.

If you are transferring binary files (most files except for READMEs and files with filename extensions such as `.txt`, `.ascii`, `.hqx`, `.ps`, `.uue`), you need to set the transfer mode as binary before starting the transfer. Use the client's Help facility for information on commands.

(2) **ftp using a Web browser** Any file in a public ftp archive can be accessed via the Web as long as you have the host name (the domain name) of the ftp server and the path. The browser takes care of the login and password conventions and also sorts out the mode of transfer (text or binary). You only need to remember to specify `ftp` (the protocol to be used) as the first part of the URL, for example `ftp://isis.cshl.org/pub/wusage/wusage3.2.tar.Z`.

Archive searching services are useful when you know what you want

There are a number of programs which search through Internet file archives, compile indexes which reference the locations of individual files, and provide a search facility on the index. The most famous of all these programs is **Archie** (Section 3.5).

Archie is a program for indexing and searching distributed information, in particular, anonymous ftp archives. Archie servers regularly generate a huge index of ftp sites all over the world and provide a search facility on that index. When you search the index, you are given a list of locations for your search string or search term. The information contained on each item indexed is fairly terse: host name, path, filesize and date, not unlike a Unix directory listing. Basically, you need to have fairly specific information (such as a filename) on what you seek in order to use Archie effectively.

Other services of similar type are also available, for instance:

- **FTP Search** `http://ftpsearch.ntnu.no/ftpsearch`;
- **Snoopie Internet Services** `http://www.snoopie.com/`.

There are also some national services providing searching of ftp servers in the one country only, for example

- **the German ASK-Sina service** `http://www.ask.uni-karlsruhe.de/asksina2/forms/WWW_Sina.html`;
- **ALLA** `http://sunsite.mff.cuni.cz/alla/` An ftp search engine for servers in the Czech Republic;
- **NoseyParker** `http://parker.vslib.cz/Parker/Netscape/parker.shtml` Another Czech search engine;
- `http://sunsite.fri.uni-lj.si:8000/ftpsearch` An FTP Search service indexing ftp servers in Slovenia;
- **FTP Search server** `http://woland.afti.nsu.ru:8000/ftpsearch` For a number of servers in the Russian Federation.

Use an ftp site near to you

Commonly, ftp sites which are heavily-used or which have a widely dispersed user group will be **mirrored**. This means that the whole structure and contents of the archive will be duplicated elsewhere. This distributes the load on the server, and makes retrieving files more efficient for users. Regular automated updating ensures that the mirror site is in step with the original collection. (See a directory of mirror collections at Imperial College, London: `http://src.doc.ic.ac.uk/Mirrors/`.)

Where there is a choice of sites offering the same software, it's usually a good idea to retrieve from the nearest site. It's faster for you and good for the network environment. For instance, if you are in Europe, give preference to a European site over an American one.

Learn how to handle compressed files and other formats

If you retrieve files from ftp archives, you will soon come across compressed and archived file formats. Compressing files, or packaging up multiple files into a single archive file, is common practice. Files take up less storage space and are quicker and easier to transfer. To compress a file requires compression software. When you retrieve such a file, you will need to have complementary decompression software to restore the file to its original form. The same principle applies with archived files and also with binary files which have been converted to text (encoded).

When you retrieve a file which has undergone one of these processes, note the file extension because this gives a clue to the software needed to restore the file to its original form (see Section 1.4.2).

1.4.1 Selected WWW software directories

ZD Net Software Library `http://www.hotfiles.com/` This library does exactly what you would expect of a library. It classifies its contents by category, and provides an informative descriptive entry on each. In fact it goes further, it also gives an evaluation of the package, which is useful if you are considering whether or not to download it. ZDNet's library lists thousands of software packages in categories such as Games, Internet, Home and Education, and so on. You can browse the archive or do a keyword search.

Shareware.com `http://www.shareware.com/` Shareware.com from C|Net includes software for PC, Mac, Unix, Amiga and Atari. You can select your operating system then run a keyword search to generate a list of entries on relevant software. Entries include size and date information on the package, and for some packages, useful descriptions as well. The site includes a list of 'Top Picks' for PC and Mac.

Jumbo `http://www.jumbo.com/` Jumbo classifies software packages into broad categories such as Internet and Intranet, Desktop publishing, Education, and so on. Within each category, programs are catalogued by operating system. Entries on each item include at least a definition, file size and date. It's possible to upload programs as well as download them. One notable feature for European users is that you are given a choice of sites from which to download.

Nerd's Heaven `http://boole.stanford.edu/nerdsheaven.html` This is not a software directory but a list of sites relevant to the task of obtaining software. It includes links to many more software directories than are mentioned here, and also links to notable archive sites for specific categories of software such as Internet, operating systems, mathematical software, software for Windows and other platforms.

1.4.2 File formats and associated software

Table 1.1 gives a few common examples of formats you may encounter and software which will handle them (though it may not be the only software which can be used).

Table 1.1 File formats and associated software.

File extension	Definition	How to process
`.exe`	Self-extracting archive for PCs	No additional software needed on a PC
`.gz`	Gnu version of zip used on Unix	Use unzip on Unix, MacGZip on Mac, Stuffit Expander for Windows on PC Windows
`.hqx`	Macintosh BinHex file encoded as text	Use Xbin on Unix, Stuffit Expander on Mac, BinHex13 on PC Windows
`.sit`	Macintosh archiving and compression format	Use Stuffit 1.51 on Unix, Stuffit Expander on Mac, Stuffit Expander for Windows on PC Windows
`.tar`	Unix archive format. Tar files may also be compressed	On Unix use command: `tar-xf`, TAR 4.0b on Mac, WinZIP on PC Windows
`.uu` or `.uue`	File converted to text format using uuencode	To convert back to original form, use command `uudecode` on Unix, uuLite 3.0 on Mac, WinCode on PC. If transferred by email, mail program may handle conversion automatically
`.Z`	Unix compressed file	To expand, use command `uncompress` on Unix if not done automatically by ftp program, Stuffit Expander with Expander Enhancer on Mac, WinZIP on PC Windows
`.zip`	pkzip PC compressed file	To expand, use Stuffit Expander w/EE on Mac, WinZIP on PC

References

Common Internet File Formats
`http://www.matisse.net/files/formats.html`

Compression FAQ
`ftp://rtfm.mit.edu/pub/usenet-by-group/comp.compression/comp.compression_Frequently_Asked_Questions_(part_1_3)`

Multimedia File Formats on the Internet
`http://ac.dat.ca/~dong/contents.html`

1.5 Communicating

For communicating with people around the world, the networks offer facilities which are hard to beat. At a purely practical level, they offer a convenient, fast and economical means of data transmission and a vast range of communication software. They also provide an environment of encouragement for the free exchange of ideas. Thus they are an effective medium through which like-minded but physically dispersed individuals and groups can meet and discuss topics of common interest. In addition, they enable people to work together though they might never find themselves in the same building. (See Section 1.6 'Group collaboration'.) And as the Internet user base steadily grows, we are likely to see much more conversing, collaborating and doing business taking place online.

1.5.1 Communicating with another person

If you would like to get in touch with someone who you know to be an Internet user, you will almost certainly be able to use **email**. When you are connected to the Internet, email allows you to send messages from your computer via the Internet to other network users cheaply and efficiently. Anyone with Internet access generally has access to email. When you get Internet access, you will normally be given a **userid** (a login name) and a password, plus an electronic mailbox, which is where your email correspondence will be deposited until you open it and read it. You use an email program on your computer to access and read email and to send messages. When you send a message it is delivered to your correspondent's mailbox and waits there until they collect it and read it. Email's flexibility, ease of use and power make it one of the most popular network services.

1.5.2 Communicating within a certain time

While email is a great system, if you need an immediate reply or if a message needs to be read by a certain time it may not be the most appropriate medium. In that case, a facility which puts you directly in touch with your correspondent may be better. The telephone is an obvious example, but as we are talking about network facilities here, it is more apt to point to **Internet phone** or even **videoconferencing** tools. These enable you to converse as you would by phone, but using the audiovisual capability of the computer rather than the telephone. In the case of videoconferencing, in addition to having sound you will see a moving picture of your correspondent (in a window) on your computer screen. With the advantage of high-speed network connections, audioconferencing and videoconferencing can provide many of the advantages of face-to-face dialogue, minus the travel costs. If you don't have a high-speed connection, and in particular if you are using an analog modem to connect, you might find facilities such as **Chat** more satisfactory. Chat enables you to exchange plain text messages with others interactively.

For more detailed information, see Section 4.4 'Real-time multimedia communication' and Section 4.5 'Collaboration tools'.

1.5.3 Group communication

If you share a common interest with a group of people who are network users, you have at your disposal an abundance of network communication facilities for pursuing that interest. First and foremost there are email-based discussion lists or **mailing lists**. These enable you to easily send one message via email to all the people who are members of the list. In turn you, as a list subscriber, will have all the messages which are sent to the list delivered to your electronic mailbox. Lists are used to exchange opinions, announce news, pose questions and provide answers, circulate information and possibly documents as well. They are an ideal medium for easy interchange by a group of people with a common interest, and for the individual, a means of overcoming the constraints of locality (where no one may be interested in the same topic) to be part of a wider and richer virtual community of common interest.

Another avenue for discussing common interests is **Usenet News**, also referred to as **News**. News encompasses some tens of thousands of interest groups (known as **newsgroups**) on almost every subject you can think of. It is widely available on the Internet, and in common with mailing lists, is an important medium for group communication. From the user's point of view, one of the major differences between mailing lists and News is that the former comes to you (that is, your mailbox) and the latter waits for you to come to it. To look at News, you need to access a News host with a Newsreader client program and from there all newsgroups on that host will be available to you until you start filtering out the ones you don't wish to see.

Web conferencing offers another medium for group discussion. It enables group members to send messages from their WWW browser to a conference without the need to install any additional software. The archives of the discussion will also be available via the Web, usually with the messages on each topic helpfully grouped together.

Mailing lists, Usenet News and Web conferencing have one thing in common. The correspondents don't need to be connected for the communication to happen. In contrast, group discussions using **Chat** take place only when people are in direct contact via the network and can converse interactively. Chat conversations at their best are spontaneous and lively and hence Chat services are widespread on the Internet. In fact there are thousands of Chat groups most notably on the system called Internet Relay Chat (IRC, see Section 4.5.3). Many of the groups are recreational, but there are also some serious discussions going on.

See Chapter 4 for more information on mailing lists, Usenet News, Web conferencing, real-time communication and collaboration tools. Refer to Section 1.2.1 to find ways to search for a mailing list or newsgroup.

1.6 Group collaboration

As the networks mature, it is increasingly obvious that they are not merely a vehicle for conveying endless amounts of information to the desktop, but can provide an effective platform for working with colleagues, irrespective of location. The use of the WWW for collaboration is currently the focus of much interest and development and many interesting new tools are appearing which make online collaborative projects a realistic, if not attractive, option for distributed workgroups. You can use the Internet for many collaborative activities such as holding meetings, ongoing discussions, working on documents, and a range of other tasks.

1.6.1 Holding meetings

Meetings with other network users using facilities such as videoconferencing are no longer a futuristic dream, especially for users on high-speed connections in the academic and research communities. And for quality communication, there is nothing quite like interactive dialogue with a person you can see and hear, even considering the benefits and convenience of tools like email. Meetings using network videoconferencing and audioconferencing enable network users to have the immediacy of face-to-face meeting. This includes the experience of real personalities, with the potential benefits of seeing spontaneous reactions, sorting out problems on the spot, getting instant feedback on ideas, not to mention savings on travel costs.

Videoconferencing and audioconferencing are powerful facilities when they work well, but not all network users have the benefit of the high-speed connections required. They may instead need to look at systems for the interactive exchange of plain-text messages such as Chat. Chat is also commonly included in collaboration software. It may not be as glamorous as phone and videoconferencing tools, but it does have the advantage of being an economical user of network resources and is therefore accessible to people on low-speed connections.

1.6.2 Discussion forums

Collaborating with others usually means ongoing discussions which ebb and flow depending on what's happening in the workgroup. Internet discussion forums provide an ideal vehicle for this type of activity. Messages can be posted to the discussion as the need arises and an archive of the discussion is usually available, enabling the group to refer back to previous messages. The software to access such forums is generally easily accessed, installed, and used.

The net excels in providing such facilities for group discussion. Mailing lists and Usenet News have a well established role here (see Section 1.5). There are many Web conferencing systems to choose from too. With these, a Web browser is used to read text messages in a forum and to add messages to the forum. Conferencing systems are organized by subject with individual conferences devoted to a particular subject. The discussion might then be further divided by discussions on particular topics, referred to as **threads**.

Collaboration tools commonly include some sort of discussion forum facility and may provide an option of setting up private conferences.

1.6.3 Working on documents

Using collaboration tools, workgroups can jointly edit common documents interactively. For instance, using a whiteboard facility, they might create a project outline for the group, each one contributing points related to their own activities. As it is amended, the display is updated on each participant's computer. When the document is complete, each person can save it for future reference. Alternatively workgroups may need to work on existing documents, for instance spreadsheets or word-processed documents, making use of application-sharing or document-sharing tools. Another option might be to have the document available on the Web and to use an annotation facility to add comments. Collaboration tools provide many possibilities for cooperative work on documents.

1.6.4 Flexible working

The activities discussed above – holding meetings, discussion forums and working on documents – can be combined with each other, and very often application software will do this for you. Collaboration suites of programs offer a range of tools in one bundle providing convenient selection of the particular combination which is useful in the circumstances. In a videoconference a workgroup might achieve results which would otherwise be out of reach without outlaying much time and money. As they talk, the participants can view and work on associated documents and graphics, revising and updating a document in response to comments and suggestions. In an education situation, a video lecture might be supplemented with complementary graphics or text, for example a manipulable 3-D graphical model, or a slide with expandable bullet points. Students may be able to use audio to ask questions. If video- or audio-conferencing are not available or give only poor quality definition, an alternative such as combining Chat with document-sharing may suffice. Many additional functions may be available such as document transfer, annotation of Web documents, group Web browsing, and so on. The important thing is to analyse your own requirements, then look for tools which might provide what you need. (Almost) anything is possible!

More information about flexible working can be found in Sections 1.5 and 4.3–4.5.

1.7 Exchanging files

The networks provide a superb transport medium for sending files to other people. They offer fast and efficient transmission over any distance, a choice of systems catering for different circumstances, and a range of application software to facilitate the transmission or distribution of files. Application software may also automatically take care of any associated processing, for instance converting binary files to text format for email transmission and converting them back to binary. When sending files, select a method and a format which suits your recipient as well as yourself.

The main options for exchanging files are discussed below.

1.7.1 Email

Using modern email packages, sending files by email is usually just a matter of selecting the menu option to attach a document to a mail message. The mailer will probably take care of the process of converting the document to plain text (ASCII) format, a necessary preliminary to sending documents via Internet email because not all mail servers through which the mail might go can handle binary formats. So, word-processed documents, spreadsheets, images and other binary files, need to be converted to plain text (ASCII) before sending. There are a number of ways in which this may be achieved:

- **MIME** MIME stands for Multipurpose Internet Mail Extensions. MIME originated because of a need to send non-ASCII documents through Internet email which, at the time, could not handle binary files. More recently though, the MIME standard has been adopted on the WWW as a method of providing some basic content description to help browsers to display content or call helper applications correctly.

MIME is incorporated into much email software. It is the preferred route for exchanging files of all types by Internet email. With a MIME-compliant mailer, information is added to the header of message specifying the type of content included in the message and also specifying how the content is encoded. Various types of content can be specified, including binary data, images, audio and video files. For example, if a GIF file is included, the mailer inserts a line like this in the header of the message:

```
Content-Type: Image/Gif
```

Though other encodings are not excluded, MIME usually uses Base64 for encoding binary files. This may be indicated in the header with a line like this:

```
Content-Transfer-Encoding: base64
```

If the receiving mailer is MIME compliant, it will correctly interpret the lines in the header and decode and display or save the file appropriately. See MIME FAQ for additional information.

- **Uuencode** Uuencode is a method of encoding binary files to plain text which originated on Unix systems, though software for other platforms is also available (see Table 1.1). Uuencode (and Uudecode) is incorporated into a number of mail packages. Exchanges between different systems using uuencode may not be entirely reliable as it has not been standardized.
- **BinHex** BinHex originated with Apple Macs and is primarily and seamlessly handled by many Mac applications, and also many PC applications such as Microsoft Internet Explorer and Netscape Navigator. Dedicated conversion software is available for a number of platforms. (See Table 1.1.)

When a message with an attached encoded document is received, the recipient's email program steps in, taking care of decoding, saving, and so on. Commonly, the message will include an icon representing the file. From there the user can select and display the file with a simple mouse click. If the email program does not have the required decoding facility it will probably save the file to some default directory leaving the user to locate and open the appropriate decoding application. This is cumbersome at the best of times, but doubly so if this is all an unfamiliar process. If you send files to people you should first establish that their mail program can handle the format you intend to use. A simple question like `Is your mail program MIME compliant?` can avoid headaches. The same considerations apply to files which are compressed as well as encoded.

Some mail systems can handle large transmissions but it is not uncommon for large files or messages sent by email to be broken down into smaller chunks. While sophisticated mail programs may handle reconstituting these adequately, a safer option for large files is to reduce the size by first compressing them, or to make them available through ftp rather than email.

1.7.2 FTP

If you have access to an ftp archive where you can place files, ftp is a good option for large numbers of files or for very large files. They can be retrieved from the archive by the recipient using ftp software (or via a Web browser) but note that ftp requires a login and password. The easiest way to get around this restriction is to place the files in an anonymous ftp archive from where they can be retrieved with the login `anonymous` and with the user's email address instead of a password. For more information about ftp see Chapter 7.

1.7.3 WWW

If you want to distribute a document to a number of people to read, converting it to HTML and putting it on a Web page may be an appropriate option (see Section 1.8 for information on how to go about it). Your correspondents need nothing more than their Web browsers to access it. This solution avoids problems associated with access from different computing platforms; sidesteps the issue of limitations of mailers; and gets around the restrictions of ftp. If the file you want to distribute is an executable or other non-readable type of file, you can still use the Web to distribute it by placing it on a Web server. It can then be accessed via its URL or via a link from a Web page containing details about the file. But note that with non-standard file types there may be an added complication. If the server doesn't recognize the file type, an entry for that file type (the MIME type) may need to be added to its configuration file. The user's browser also can be configured to recognize the file type if desired However, if files come from an unknown source, it is generally considered more secure to save to disk initially. See further information on tools for security and encryption in Chapter 6.

Irrespective of the variations which non-standard file types introduce, using the WWW to make files available to others has much to recommend it.

1.8 WWW publishing

The World Wide Web is a great enabler, not just for bringing information *to* the desktop, but for distributing information *from* the desktop to the world. It effectively realizes the truism that 'on the Internet, anyone can be a publisher'! There has never been a medium which gave ordinary folk the power to publish to the world at large so easily and economically, which provided a ready-made vehicle for reproduction and distribution, which effortlessly reached other countries and cultures, which made light of status or organizational hierarchy, and which was so enthusiastically received. It is little wonder that the WWW is growing at a phenomenal rate. Who, with something to say, could resist being part of this information mainstream?

1.8.1 Producing Web documents

Publishing your information on the WWW can be done relatively cheaply and easily. The normal format for WWW documents is HTML (HyperText Markup Language) though other formats can also be viewed with additional software (see the information on plug-ins in the Glossary). Files in any format can be made available on the Web leaving the user to handle the details of viewing or processing (see Section 1.7 'Exchanging files' for further discussion). The essence of WWW publishing is that you produce HTML documents and place them on a Web server on the network. The documents can then be accessed from anywhere on the network. Once in place, you will need to maintain your site.

HTML

HTML is like a hidden layer behind the document that you see in a Web browser. It is, as its name implies, a **markup language**. Marking up text is like issuing instructions on how the text should be interpreted and displayed. In the case of HTML, the instructions come in the form of HTML **elements**, or **tags**. The Web browser displays a document as instructed by the HTML. HTML tags do a number of things, such as the following:

- **define the structure of a document**, for example the HEAD (information about the document) and BODY (the main part of the document which is displayed by the browser)

```
<HEAD>
<TITLE>Title of the document</TITLE>
</HEAD>
<BODY>
This is the main body of the document.
</BODY>
```

- **indicate features of the appearance**, for example white background and blue text

```
<BODY BACKGROUND="WHITE" TEXT="BLUE">
```

- **indicate formatting of text,** for example text in italics

```
<I>HTML elements</I>
```

- **indicate the presence and position of graphics,** for example show the image file `box.gif` here and place it on the left of the page

```
<IMG SRC="box.gif" ALIGN="LEFT">
```

To see some HTML, you can use your browser's View menu at the top of the screen and select Source or Page source. This will show the HTML of the page you are currently viewing.

To see the range of tags available with HTML, refer to a list such as the *Compendium of HTML Elements* at `http://www.uni-siegen.de/help/html/compendium` or the more terse *Bare Bones Guide to HTML* at `http://werbach.com/barebones/` by Kevin Werbach (available in a number of languages).

HTML files are plain-text (ASCII) files. The filename will have the extension `.html` or `.htm`.

There are many programs which can help in generating HTML documents and also, a number of the programs we are accustomed to using (such as word processors) now include a function for automatically generating HTML. See Section 5.1 'WWW authoring' for further discussion of tools and techniques.

Generating Web documents is not merely a technical exercise. Good style and good practice have an impact on the quality and usability of pages. Check out the Bibliography for useful guides for Web authors which cover issues of style, as well as HTML.

Graphics

Graphics are an important feature of Web pages, illustrating, enhancing and complementing text. Files in GIF and JPEG formats can be automatically displayed by graphical Web browsers. Other formats such as animation, movie and 3-D files too can be viewed with additional software. Generating graphics has become an essential aspect of all-round Web development, and in some contexts, is the dominant aspect. Graphics skills and graphics applications are standard items in the Web toolkit, just as HTML authoring and HTML editors are. For further information see Section 5.2 'Graphics in Web pages'.

Interactivity in Web pages

Web pages come alive with interactive functionality with the aid of programming and scripting languages. See Section 5.3 'Interactive Web pages' with associated discussions of some of the currently available tools.

1.8.2 The Web server

A Web server is a program which makes Web documents available to Web browsers on request (another example of an Internet client–server relationship – see the Glossary). Web server software is available for many different computers and operating systems, though working servers normally run on high-end workstations which can handle multiple transactions simultaneously. On a networked Web server, your Web documents can be accessed from anywhere on the network.

To have access to space on a Web server, you will need to have an account (login and password). With this in place, you will be able to transfer (ftp) your completed HTML and graphics files to your directory on the server.

1.8.3 Maintaining your site

There is a lot of out-of-date information and dead links on the Web. *Don't add to it!* Keep your information current. Check hypertext links regularly to make sure they still work. There are tools available for doing such housekeeping tasks automatically.

Usage statistics are an important aspect of maintenance. They will tell you, for instance, if anyone is accessing the information you are providing or if they encountered errors in finding any of the files you linked to.

See the WWW authoring section of the Bibliography for a list of useful references.

1.9 Keeping up to date

Keeping up to date with what's happening on the Internet is well beyond the resources of any individual, but fortunately there are services which monitor and alert users to new developments and new services, and also to changed information.

The Internet is also a great source for keeping current with general news about events at home and abroad. As well as the obvious sources of online newspaper and magazines, there are many news alerting services, some of which can be customized to fit your interests. A number of search engines offer news sections in addition to their main service.

The use of intelligent agents to generate personalized news on a regular basis means that users can exercise control over the information that comes to them, rather than be the passive recipients of a pre-determined selection of news from a remote server. Agent software such as Autonomy Agentware or Quarterdeck's WebCompass may be installed on the user's machine and instructed on what to search for and how often. The agent may make its own decisions on where to go to find the required information.

Some relevant sources are described below.

Current events

PointCast http://www.pointcast.com/ PointCast Inc. offers a free personalized news and information service via the Internet, offering six 'channels' covering news, companies, industries, weather, sports and lifestyles. Its free software which works with Netscape can be installed on a local computer and will go into action when the computer is not in use – news is displayed in the screen saver.

Infoseek's News sections http://www.infoseek.com/ Searches the Web for news items or news wires, newspapers or Usenet newsgroups. It can also personalize your news pages and have news delivered to you daily by email.

Lycos http://www.lycos.com/ Provides a Top News section.

Excite http://www.excite.com/ Provides News Tracker and the opportunity to personalize your own news pages (set up a News Tracker account).

New Internet resources

Yahoo What's New http://www.yahoo.com/new/ Links to new entries of interest in Yahoo database.

Net-happenings http://www.mid.net:80/NET/ Announcements of interest to network support staff and end users.

In Site http://www.mcs.com/~jcr/INSITE.html New Internet sites of value particularly to librarians.

Scout Report http://wwwscout.cs.wisc.edu/scout/report/ New and newly discovered Internet resources and network tools of interest to researchers and educators.

Internet Resources Newsletter http://www.hw.ac.uk/libWWW/irn/irn.html Descriptive listing of new sites (not searchable).

Changed Internet resources

URL-minder http://www.netmind.com/URL-minder/URL-minder.html Keeps track of nominated Internet resources and sends you email whenever the content changes.

Commercial agent software

Autonomy Agentware http://www.agentware.com
Quarterdeck Corporation's WebCompass http://www.quarterdeck.com

1.10 Self-protection

The Internet is not necessarily a jungle, but it may not be an entirely benign place either. It is a good idea to be aware of the basic ways in which you can protect your privacy and your data and at the same time contribute to the Internet's security infrastructure. Many of the big security issues in the Internet have to be left to system and network administrators and other technical people. But at the grass roots level, security is a general issue which implies responsibilities for all computer and network users. It is as much about everyday security precautions like keeping your password secure as it is about sophisticated anti-hacking measures such as encryption, digital signatures, and so on. Section 1.11 on Netiquette provides a few guidelines on maintaining the security of your account.

1.10.1 Email

Note that email is not a secure medium since it often involves sending clear text messages through unknown computers which may be operated and managed by untrusted third parties. If you need to send sensitive information, it is advisable to use some form of encryption and, optionally, authentication. See Chapter 6 for information on this.

1.10.2 The Web

While users can roam the network retrieving information, information can be collected from them too, with or without this being obvious. Web servers can retrieve for their log files details of the Internet Provider's address, the computer's host name, the previous URL accessed and input to forms (when the GET command is used).

New WWW tools embedded in Web pages vastly extend the possibilities for interaction with the user and the user's computer.

- **Java and Javascript** extend the functionality of Web pages but are not entirely without risk because they execute scripts or programs on the user's computer. They may be seen as potential risks though there are built-in safeguards, particularly with Java, which has security limits imposed by restricting the behaviour of Java applets to a set of safe actions.
- **ActiveX** controls are not confined in this way but can come with a digital signature so that their source is known and possibly certified by some authority. Before the browser downloads an unsigned ActiveX control it warns the user so that he or she can opt to abort the transfer.
- Users are often required to provide details about themselves in order to register for online services or to make purchases. **Cookies** are a device (stored on the user's computer) used to record this type of information so that it is available to the server in future.

These tools add to the functionality of the Web, but fortunately can be turned off if they seem to impose too great a risk to security or privacy. For more information refer to Section 5.3.

While there are built-in safeguards with these new tools, familiar formats may pose risks as well. Automatically running executable programs downloaded via the Internet can present a risk because a program may contain a malicious script which corrupts or deletes files. Examples of executables might be something as apparently innocuous as spreadsheets containing macros or word processor style sheets. It's best to check the source of origin of the program if possible, or look at it carefully before running it.

1.11 Netiquette

In essence, Netiquette, or network etiquette, is all about maintaining a good network environment, that is, a good technical environment in which things function efficiently and an orderly social environment in which people can work effectively. To practise good network etiquette, users need to have a general awareness of the impact of their actions on other network users and on the network itself and to be considerate in their use of the network. This section aims to build awareness of some of the major sensitive areas and to suggest relevant guidelines for good network etiquette. Additional material on netiquette can be found on Arlene Rinaldi's *The Net: User Guidelines and Etiquette* at `http://www.fau.edu/rinaldi/net/index.htm`.

The 'Ten Commandments For Computer Ethics' from the Computer Ethics Institute provide a good general starting point for any network user (see Section 1.11.6). On the subject of rules, it is also worth mentioning that networks usually have some form of Acceptable Use Policy (AUP). Observe the policy of your own network. Infringing the rules may result in your account being withdrawn. Networks may specifically prohibit the use of the network for creation or transmission of material which is illegal, defamatory, offensive, obscene or indecent. Academic networks will probably prohibit the use of the network for commercial purposes. A chastening thought is the fact that much network traffic is likely to cross the boundaries of a number of networks and possibly countries before it reaches its destination and that each will have a different AUP and different laws. This suggests that it is better to play it safe on the networks.

1.11.1 Security

First, some general guidelines relating to maintaining the security of your account (that is, your login and password on an Internet host, and associated access to filespace, electronic mailbox and Web space). Users rely on system managers to a large extent to take care of the overall security and integrity of the system. However, if hackers are intent on breaking in, any weakness in the system can provide an initial entry point. This can be provided by a single user who is slack about the security of his or her id and password.

(1) Keep your password secret. Don't give it to anyone else, and especially, don't include login and password details in an email message.
(2) Use a password which can't be guessed or found in a dictionary. Recommended practice is to make it a mixture of letters and numbers, upper case and lower case.
(3) Change your password frequently. Normal computer security is important for network security. Network login details may be obtained from your computer if it falls into the wrong hands.
(4) Keep your computer secure. Don't leave a machine on which you are logged in unattended.

1.11.2 Abiding by the law

Libel

Don't use the network to make damaging or untruthful statements about others.

Copyright

Respect intellectual property. Don't use or distribute copyright material as if it were your own, and always obtain permission if you plan to use someone else's material. This applies whether it is text, sound, video, graphics files or programs.

Obscenity

In most cases, users will be bound by the AUP of their network in areas such as obscenity and pornography. If not the network provider, then the country's law may apply to the provision or transmission of this type of material. Unfortunately, the interest of a minority of network users in pornographic and obscene material is a dominant factor in the general perception of the Internet, a shadow which falls over all Internet users.

1.11.3 Use of resources

Computing resources are finite, and busy servers can become overloaded. If a server's primary role is to supply local needs, outside users may have restrictions imposed upon them, which is reasonable considering that the use of free services on a network is not a right but a privilege. Network capacity is also a finite resource though bandwidth overall is constantly being increased. Generally, economical use of network resources helps to promote efficiency all round.

(1) Always comply with requests to limit use. For instance, ftp archive sites may discourage outside use during office hours.
(2) When you are connected to a network host, for instance via telnet or an ftp client, you are tying up resources which are then unavailable to anyone else. Limit your connection sessions to a minimum and logout as soon as possible.
(3) For preference, select a location nearest to you when accessing information which is available from a number of sites. Such good practice helps to ease the pressure on overloaded transoceanic links. Fortunately there is an increasing trend for important services originating in the USA (for example, a number of Web search engines) to be mirrored in Europe and elsewhere.

1.11.4 Email

Because of email's special characteristics, it is especially important to observe good etiquette in using it. These special characteristics are its speed, immediacy and ease of use. It is all too easy to dash off an angry message, press the Send button, and have your correspondent reading it almost instantly. Copy the message to a mailing list and without any additional effort, you will have managed to offend all the list members as well. (Read more about offending ways with email in the Emily Postnews document at `http://www.clari.net/brad/emily.html`.) The following are a few guidelines which may help to steer a safe path between the pitfalls:

(1) Keep messages concise, clear and polite.
(2) Never send an email when angry or upset.
(3) Send plain-text messages only, avoiding tabs and control characters.
(4) Confer with your correspondent before sending him or her an encoded file by email. Mail programs may automatically decode encoded files, but they don't all handle the same formats with equal efficiency.
(5) Always insert a subject line. Subject lines are a great boon in the management of email.
(6) Smileys are an accepted convention in email messages. You can use them to help convey your message if words fail you. For example,

    :-) [I'm pleased about this or this is a joke]
    :-([this is sad, regrettable, I'm sorry about it]

(7) Make a basic check of outgoing messages before despatching them. Check for spelling and clarity and check the 'To:' field (is it addressed to the intended recipient?).

Not exactly a point of etiquette, but a point to remember for your own protection is that email is not a secure medium in its regular form. It is possible, though not probable, that messages could be read along the way to their destination by system managers or others with access privileges. Therefore, don't put confidential or sensitive information in an email message. If you need to transmit messages securely, you should investigate email encryption. Naturally your correspondent will need to do likewise. One of the widely used encryption programs currently used is PGP (Pretty Good Privacy), described in Section 6.4.

1.11.5 Group communication

Group communication adds an extra dimension to these basic guidelines on email. Netiquette becomes even more important. Without it the group environment can become a very uncivilized place. A few guidelines follow which can be applied equally to mailing lists or newsgroups.

(1) When you compose a message to send to a group forum, assume that it will be received by a busy person who is pressed for time and has a mountain of correspondence to work through. Therefore, always be economical and focused in your group correspondence.
(2) Keep to the topic of the list or newsgroup.
(3) Provide a subject line with your message.
(4) Familiarize yourself with the environment of the group before contributing; read any FAQs, get an idea of the sorts of discussions which take place, ascertain the level.
(5) Be polite.
(6) When soliciting information, ask people to reply to you personally and later provide a summary of responses for the list.

Spamming

Spamming refers to the practice of flooding a network service in an indiscriminate and inappropriate fashion such as the mass posting of an email message or newsgroup article to large numbers of lists or newsgroups, irrespective of whether it is related to the topic. Unfortunately, with the onrush of commercial interests on the Internet, spamming is becoming more common. Junk mail and irritation are the results. Recipients can respond by forwarding the message plus a complaint to `postmaster@<domain name of message sender>`. (Strip the username off any address and insert `postmaster` before the `@` sign.) Amend the subject line as appropriate.

1.11.6 The Ten Commandments For Computer Ethics

(from the Computer Ethics Institute)

(1) Thou shalt not use a computer to harm other people.
(2) Thou shalt not interfere with other people's computer work.
(3) Thou shalt not snoop around in other people's files.
(4) Thou shalt not use a computer to steal.
(5) Thou shalt not use a computer to bear false witness.
(6) Thou shalt not use or copy software for which you have not paid.
(7) Thou shalt not use other people's computer resources without authorization.
(8) Thou shalt not appropriate other people's intellectual output.
(9) Thou shalt think about the social consequences of the program you write.
(10) Thou shalt use a computer in ways that show consideration and respect.

2 Exploring the Networks

The exploring tools covered in this chapter provide a means of browsing through a wide range of network resources in a uniform and intuitive way. These tools, with their simple point and click interface enhanced by attractive graphical formatting, have helped to fire the enthusiasm of users as well as the imagination of software developers, and to advance the ongoing revolution in the use and application of networked information.

The reigning monarch in this kingdom is surely the World Wide Web. Not only is the Web a superb tool for network exploration, but it constantly amasses new functions and capabilities. It has colonized most other network tools and integrated their functionality into its own all-enveloping interface to such an extent that the only essential network tool for many users is a Web browser.

Amongst the tools which the World Wide Web has effectively absorbed is gopher, that pioneer tool for browsing network information. Most users will access gopher resources with a Web browser, and are unlikely to require a special-purpose gopher client. However, there is still a considerable amount of information available on gopher servers, and this chapter would not be complete without covering gopher.

2.1 The World Wide Web

The **World Wide Web**, also called the **WWW** or simply the **Web**, is a hypermedia information system providing seamless access to distributed information on the Internet and a flexible means of publishing information.

Hypermedia

Hypermedia (or hypertext, if it is text only) documents are ones which contain embedded links (hyperlinks) to other related documents in any media. The link information is hidden from view, but its presence may be indicated to the reader by special formatting of the linked text or graphics. This link information includes the unique Internet address of the referenced document, that is, its URL (Uniform Resource Locator). The format which makes it possible to embed this information invisibly is HTML (HyperText Markup Lanuage), the standard format for Web documents.

Further details of URLs can be found in the Glossary. HTML is described in Section 1.8.

When a hyperlink is selected, the document to which it refers is immediately fetched and displayed for the user. This document may contain links to further documents. Thus the user can track related concepts from one document to another, traversing the net in a seamless fashion, regardless of the physical location of the documents or the type of computers on which they are held.

Hyperlinking offers advantages for Web authors as well as readers. By offering optional levels of enrichment and enhancement of document content through links to related documents, it adds value and context to Web documents with an immediacy seldom possible with traditional forms of information.

Links in Web documents span not only the universe of networked information but also the range of media because the Web is a **multimedia** system encompassing text, audio, video, graphics and other types of files.

Distributed information

Through the WWW, the user can access documents distributed across hundreds of thousands of servers all over the world. Consult a summary of the list of registered servers (see 'Finding more information' below) to get an idea of the geographical range of WWW servers. In an Intranet the physical range may be confined to one campus or even one building. Whichever it is, the end result is similar. The WWW interface makes it appear that there is one integrated corpus of documents, one massive file system, when in fact the files are held on many separate computers.

Publishing information

The WWW provides an easy, platform-independent, supremely flexible means of making information available. It is easy because WWW documents are normally written in HTML, the rudiments of which are easily learnt, and for which there are many editors and conversion programs available. Documents in standard HTML can be read by any Web browser on any platform. Distribution of the information worldwide becomes just a matter of making potential users aware of it, and revision and updating of the information is managed by maintaining the files at the source of distribution, namely, on the server.

Access

Access with a client

Users access the Web with client software, normally referred to as a **Web browser**. As with other Internet client–server systems, the browser (the local *client*) interacts with a remote *server*. The server has the information to give out. The browser has the task of requesting, fetching and displaying the information on behalf of the user. Many Web browsers for different platforms are available. At the no-frills end of the spectrum are plain text browsers such as **Lynx** which runs under Unix and VMS. The most popular browsers are high-end graphical browsers such as **Netscape Navigator** (Netscape Communications, part of the Communicator suite) and **Internet Explorer** (Microsoft), both of which are available for PC Windows and Apple Mac. Versions of Netscape for the various flavours of Unix are also available. **Mosaic** was the first graphical browser to gain widespread usage, but currently the bulk of Web users use either Netscape or Internet Explorer. While these two browsers are developing into massive all-encompassing Internet tools trailing plug-in and add-on programs in their wake, there is a reverse trend in specific areas such as the development of trimmed-down browsers for hand-held devices. For details on some of the popular browsers see the Appendix.

Standard functions of browsers

A number of standard functions can be expected with a graphical Web browser:

- enabling the user to follow links in the current document to other Web documents,
- enabling the user to follow links to other Internet information systems such as gopher and ftp,
- opening local documents,
- saving retrieved documents,
- printing the current document,
- maintaining a history of visited URLs,
- providing a facility for moving back and forward between URLs visited in the current session,
- viewing the source (the HTML) of the current document,
- maintaining a file of URLs which the user wishes to record,
- searching for a term in the current document,
- handling forms,
- displaying images (GIF, JPEG formats) inline,
- handling links from imagemaps,
- maintaining a store (cache) of visited pages for re-use where appropriate,
- enabling the user to configure preferences for:

  - the home (starting) page
  - the appearance of documents
  - whether or not to automatically load images
  - which helper applications to use
  - use of a proxy server.

More recently added configuration options include:

- how to handle documents containing Java applets, scripts, or cookies (see Section 5.3),
- whether to use authentication certificates or not,
- preventing access to sites with unacceptable content rating.

Accessing a specific URL

Following embedded links in Web documents offers a convenient ready-made exploration trail. But it is also possible to tell the browser to go to a specific URL. A menu item such as File – Open Location or Open File (GO with Lynx) is normally available, and will generate a prompt for keying in the desired URL.

Accessing email and Usenet News with a Web browser

As the leading Web browsers have developed they have absorbed more and more functions until they have arrived at a point where they effectively fill the role of all-purpose Internet tools. Most users expect that their Web browser will have email and Usenet News functionality, though they may not necessarily use it. If they do, it is a simple matter of selecting the appropriate menu item or button in the browser's window. This usually generates a separate Mail or News window from which most basic functions of a dedicated mail or News program are available.

Accessing the Web with email

For users who have only email access to the Internet, or for other users who grow impatient with download time, there is the option of accessing Web pages via email. An email request for a URL is sent to a WWW-mail server which then fetches the document from the WWW server, and returns it to the requester in an email message.

For further information and a current list of WWW-mail servers, consult *Accessing The Internet By E-Mail: Doctor Bob's Guide to Offline Internet Access* at `ftp://ftp.mailbase.ac.uk/pub/lists/lis-iis/files/e-access-inet.txt`.

Accessing the Web with telnet

The W3 Consortium (see 'Finding more information' below) maintains a list of telnet-accessible Web browsers at `http://www.w3.org/hypertext/WWW/FAQ/Bootstrap.html`.

Coverage

There are millions of host computers on the Internet and the World Wide Web effectively encompasses all of the information they make publicly available. As well as files on hundreds of thousands of WWW servers, the Web also embraces files on other Internet information systems, such as gopher and ftp. Web servers and browsers understand and can use the protocols of these other systems as well as the Web's native protocol, HTTP (HyperText Transfer Protocol). For example, files in ftp archives can be accessed by specifying the appropriate URL which will begin with `ftp`, such as:

```
ftp://src.doc.ic.ac.uk/pub/index.txt
```

The document `index.txt` would then be displayed by the Web browser, albeit in plain-text format.

The main systems with which the Web interacts in this way are gopher, ftp, telnet, wais, mail and news.

Using

Basic uses

Most users readily grasp the idea of how to use the World Wide Web. Following links is usually a matter of pointing and clicking. The other main action in using the Web is filling in data in forms (see the Glossary for more information). Where the Web is used as a front-end for some other application, such as a database, the user can be prompted for search terms via a form on the Web page. The search terms keyed into the form are then passed to the database, the query is processed by the database, and the results passed back and output as a freshly generated HTML page containing the search results. This is the system used by Web search engines.

Added interactivity

Additional interactivity is provided through the Java programming language and through scripting languages such as Javascript (see Sections 5.3.2 and 5.3.3). Java applets, that is, small Java programs, can be included in Web pages and used to run certain processes on the local machine. For instance, Java could be used to help guide the user in framing a complex database search, providing feedback and advice interactively as the user keys in the search, all this is done locally, cutting out inefficient use of server and network resources.

Handling additional file types

The standard role of Web browsers is to access and display HTML documents. Browsers interpret the HTML tags and display the document accordingly. They can also retrieve and display other types of files if they recognize the file type (MIME type – see Section 1.7) and have the software available to handle it. The software may be built into the browser, for example certain image file types (GIF and JPEG) are displayed by graphical browsers as an integral part of the document. Other file types may require some extra software, commonly programs designed to work in conjunction with a browser for the display of a specific file type (plug-ins), or possibly stand-alone programs which the browser can launch to handle certain file types (**helper applications**). Another technology employed to extend the functionality of Web documents is Microsoft's ActiveX technology for PC Windows. Amongst other things, ActiveX allows non-HTML documents such as Microsoft Excel or Word files to be viewed through a Web browser while automatically taking care of the associated software requirements.

Keeping track of useful resources
With millions of resources available, identifying and finding useful material can be a problem. One important information management tool for the Web is the **bookmark** facility provided by Web browsers (also known as **Favorites** (Internet Explorer) or a **hot list**). Bookmarks enable users to keep track of Web resources which they find useful. Some browsers provide for more advanced bookmark management with a facility for hierarchical grouping of annotated bookmarks. The list of bookmarks is in effect a personalized, needs-based view of the online information universe.

Examples

The WWW is now a densely populated place and new sites proliferate at a dramatic rate. The Web has a presence in most corners of human activity, ranging from recreation to education, from scientific research to commercial transactions, and most areas in between. On the Web you can buy a house, find a job, book a cruise, check out weather maps, browse a local newspaper, look at a medieval manuscript or take a tour of the solar system. The most interesting sites are of course the ones which contain information which is pertinent to the user's interests or concerns – sites which offer solutions to problems, commercial advantage, information which is otherwise unavailable, or just plain convenience. For instance, the Web might be used to look up a list of local medical practitioners, which movies are showing in town this evening, the price of company X's shares, whether the parcel you sent today has reached its destination.

If you are interested in the techniques being used, you can see examples of database searching using forms and CGI, animation (viewable with Shockwave), sound, video and 3-D graphics. There are journals online with the look of conventionally published journals (viewed with Adobe Acrobat), scrolling, jumping and rotating graphics, courtesy of Javascript, images which constantly change (often these are animated gifs). You can see how Java is being used for business purposes, and the use of artificial intelligence techniques in predicting your musical tastes. There is an increasing trend to relate the information on the Web to the interests and preferences of the individual. From the user's point of view those information slaves, 'intelligent agents' (Section 3.6), hold the promise of exercising some control over one's own information environment, but at the same time, automatic processes may be stealthily gathering information about the individual to be later used for unknown purposes, but most likely direct marketing.

One important and increasing trend is the use of the Web as a collaborative tool. Mailing lists (Section 4.1) and newsgroups are standard sources, but computer supported collaborative work via the Web is equally feasible. See Section 4.5 for more details.

Finding more information

- **World Wide Web Consortium site** `http://www.w3.org` The World Wide Web Consortium (W3C) is an international industry consortium which seeks to develop common standards for the evolution of the World Wide Web. These standards are issued as **W3C Recommendations** and supported for industry-wide adoption by Consortium members. The W3C also develops applications to demonstrate use of new technology, and a reference code implementation to embody and promote standards. It maintains a repository of information about the World Wide Web for developers and users, including well-known resource listings such as:
  - **World Wide Web Virtual Library** `http://www.w3.org/pub/DataSources/bySubject/`
  - **W3 Servers** `http://www.w3.org/pub/DataSources/WWW/Servers.html`
- **RFCs** `http://ds.internic.net/ds/dspg1intdoc.html` RFCs (Request for Comments) are the standards developed by the working groups of the IETF (Internet Engineering Task Force). They define the protocols on which the Internet operates and constitute a primary reference source on any technical aspect of the Internet, including the WWW.
- **WWW FAQ** `http://www.boutell.com/faq/` Maintained by Thomas Boutell and mirrored at a number of sites, the WWW FAQ (Frequently Asked Questions) answers basic questions about the Web, including information on obtaining browsers for a number of platforms such as Amiga, NeXT, VM/CMS, Acorn and others.
- **Web forums**
  - **W3C Mailing lists** `http://www.w3.org/pub/WWW/Mail/Lists.html`
  - **HTML Groups, Discussion Forums and Archives** `http://www.w3.org/pub/WWW/MarkUp/Forums`

2.2 Gopher

Gopher is a networked information retrieval system which offers a menu interface to Internet information. Menus are usually hierarchically nested, and may list items of many different types, for instance, directories, text files, picture or sound files. Gopher menus not only list information on gopher servers, but they may also include items from other Internet information systems such as WAIS index searches or telnet sessions. Gopher menus present an integrated and consistent interface to information located on many different Internet servers.

Access

Like WWW and other Internet tools, gopher is a client–server system. Gopher information is held by gopher servers, and is accessed by clients using the gopher protocol. Dedicated gopher client software may be used, but currently the most common route of access is via a WWW browser which uses the gopher protocol, for example Netscape or Internet Explorer.

Dedicated gopher client software for many different platforms has been developed and links to sources may be found at `gopher://boombox.micro.umn.edu:70/11/gopher`. Be aware, however, that software may no longer be supported or developed.

Some sites make plain terminal-based gopher clients available for public use. These can be accessed via telnet. A list is available from `gopher://gopher.tc.umn.edu/` by selecting the menu item Terminal Based Information.

Gopher information can also be accessed by email through the gateway service. For details, see *Accessing The Internet By E-Mail: Doctor Bob's Guide to Offline Internet Access* at `ftp://ftp.mailbase.ac.uk/pub/lists/lis-iis/files/e-access-inet.txt`.

Coverage

With the advance of the WWW, gopher's use has declined dramatically. There were previously hundreds of gopher servers worldwide registered and listed by the Gopher Consultant Service at the University of Minnesota's Computer and Information Services Department. The list is still available from `gopher://gopher.tc.umn.edu/` by selecting the menu items Other Gopher and Information Servers or All the Gopher Servers in the World. But visiting gopherspace now is like straying into the land that time forgot, and though there is the occasional currently maintained gopher server, many are no longer operational.

Using

Selecting and retrieving items from gopher menus is simply done, usually with a mouse double-click, or on a terminal interface, by typing the selected menu item number.

Gopher is a plain-text tool, so when files of types other than plain text are accessed, helper applications need to be launched to view the file or to access the service. For instance, a picture file in gif format will require the use of a graphical application which displays gifs, or a link to a telnet session will require a telnet application to be launched. Gopher clients may be configured to launch the appropriate application automatically.

Most gopher clients provide a bookmark facility, allowing users to keep track of items they might wish to revisit. Bookmarks are presented in the form of a customized gopher menu.

Searching gopher

Gopher menus may be searched using a tool called **Veronica**. The currently operational veronica servers may be accessed from the University of Minnesota Gopher by selecting the menus Other Gopher and Information Servers or Search Titles in Gopherspace using Veronica. From there, the user is prompted to supply a keyword and the search is then run on the veronica server's index. Note that veronica indexes gopher titles only. It does not search in the text of documents. Help on searching is available from the veronica server menu.

Examples

The University of Minnesota Gopher provides links to many different types of services, such as libraries, news, discussion groups, ftp archives, search services, telnet sessions. Its link to Other Gopher and Information Servers offers not only geographic listings of gopher servers, but also links to search facilities such as veronica and WAIS.

Finding more information

From the University of Minnesota Gopher, select Information about Gopher.

3 Searching Tools

Computer networks represent an online information cornucopia, a vast and overflowing supply of information augmented every day with yet more rich offerings. But without searching tools, this huge mass of information becomes almost inpenetrable. Searching tools enable us to extract from the online mass the precise and particular information we need.

- **Web search tools** provide a means of searching the WWW and other information systems.
- **Directory services** provide structured databases of information on people and other entities.
- **Archie** is a pioneer tool for searching Internet file archives.
- **Intelligent agents** automatically carry out personalized searches for users.

With the proliferation of information on the WWW, effective searching facilities are a vital item in every Internet user's toolkit. Locating required information on the Internet is more and more dependent on the effective use of these search services. If used effectively, they provide a bridge between users and the information they require and thus add value to online information resources. But as the search services themselves proliferate, users presented with a bewildering array of possibilities want to know how their information requirements can best be met. They have at their disposal search engines, meta-search services, specialist search facilities, subject directories and subject gateways, all of which are different, both individually and collectively. It would be misleading to suggest that there is normally one cure-all solution to any given problem. Two broad approaches are suggested.

Firstly, employing a variety of tactics can often be a productive strategy, and many of the search services have recognized this fact. For instance, complementary directory listings are added to search engine services, and search facilities are offered with directories. Notable also as an example of throwing all the available tools at the problem are the meta-search services which enable users to search multiple indexes simultaneously.

Secondly, for a complex, closely specified search, the alternative approach of fine tuning can yield dividends. Mapping out the structure of the search helps to pinpoint the particular search features which will be needed. For instance, it may be obvious that Boolean searching will be required, or that only the current year's information will be useful. In these types of cases, identifying search services which offer these features is a useful exercise.

3.1 Web search engines

In essence, Web search engines are programs which search databases of World Wide Web and other Internet information. They are accessed via a search form on a Web page. The user types into the form some words describing what he or she is looking for, the search engine searches through its database for information which seems to match what's required and returns a list of matching resources. The list of matches is usually ranked according to how well they seem to satisfy the search, and each list entry includes a hypertext link to the actual resource it references. A relevance score may also be given.

The search engine proper is complemented by a program which gathers information for its database. These types of programs are commonly referred to as **robots**, **spiders** or **crawlers**. They trawl through the Internet, automatically retrieving data from one site after another for inclusion in their database. Normally hypertext links within one document will provide a list of the next sites to link to and pull data from, and these sites will have more hypertext links to follow, and so the process goes on continuously. Robots can assemble huge databases of information, but gathered indiscriminately.

Many of the search engines have a complementary directory listing of resources, grouped by subject, and may offer the option of searching this as well as the robot-generated database.

While Web search services have these basic processes in common, there are many respects in which they differ from each other, and it is these differences which will impact on users, on their ability to specify searches precisely and on their chances of finding relevant information.

3.1.1 User requirements

While users undoubtedly have a myriad of different search requirements, overall there are a number of qualities which may promote the chance of successful searching. These include:

- ease of use,
- comprehensiveness,
- quality of content,
- control over the search,
- flexibility in searching,

- valid assessment of relevance,
- informative presentation of results.

Ease of use

Web search services generally provide a simple entry point via a single window for keyword input. Advanced searching options may provide multiple input windows, with drop-down menu selection of operators for combining search terms. Additional options on the home page often include links to directory listings, company directories, Web FAQs, news stories, specialist searching services such as White Pages services, Usenet News searching, and so on. There is immense variety and choice, so much so that these added extras can overwhelm the simple search window. The necessary evil of jumping, hopping and skipping advertisements, a major source of income for commercial search services, adds to the busy look of the pages. When the user does sort out where the search input window is, it is generally easy and straightforward to use.

Comprehensiveness

At a basic level, bigger is obviously better, all other things being equal. The larger search services such as AltaVista, Lycos, Excite and Infoseek index some tens of millions of Web documents. Most search engines provide information on the current tally of their database. Such tallies quickly go out of date so it is as well to check the current documentation for really current information. Apart from the impressive tallies of documents indexed, other questions may be asked, such as: how are the resources counted? Possibilities include:

- only the URLs of pages whose full text is indexed are counted. Excite claims to do this. (See Excite's document *How to count URLs* `http://www.excite.com/ice/counting.html`);
- all the URL tags in an indexed page are included in the count even when the resources are never retrieved and indexed. Excite claims that this method is used by Lycos;
- URLs are counted every time they are linked to and retrieved, even if this occurs many times. Excite claims that this method is used by OpenText.

A further question might be: what is the scope of the database? Are areas other than the Web covered, for example News, gopher, ftp?

- Excite covers the WWW, reviewed sites and News;
- Infoseek Ultra covers the WWW, News and FAQs;
- AltaVista covers the WWW and News;
- Lycos covers the WWW, Gopher and FTP;
- OpenText covers the WWW.

Finally, what information is indexed? A limited number of Web search services actually index the full text of Internet resources. Such indexes are generally enormous and require substantial computing resources to maintain. In theory, they give access to all the information contained in a document, whether or not on the main topic of the document. AltaVista, InfoSeek, Excite and OpenText index the full text. Lycos indexes the URL, title, headings, significant words and part of the text.

Quality of content

The currency of the information in the database is an important aspect of quality. Currency in this context relates to information content, and also to the ever-present question for all maintainers of Web services – do the links still work? For Web search services, a useful feature is frequent updating and verification of items in the database. A number of search engines, for example AltaVista and Infoseek Ultra, revisit URLs at a variable rate depending on how often changes are made to the page.

Control over the search

The treatment of search terms

- How are multiple search terms combined? Default of AND or OR.

Most commonly the default is OR. For instance if your search terms were:

```
training guide dogs blind
```

the search engine with this default would search for documents which contained `training` OR `guide` OR `dogs` OR `blind`, giving an enormous list of matches, many of which might not be at all relevant. Ranking of matches according to how well they are deemed to satisfy the search may offset the apparent disadvantages of this approach. Lycos's Simple Search employs this approach. When the alternative approach of having the search terms joined with AND is used, the list of matches would rank first documents which contained all of the search terms.

- Is full Boolean searching provided for, that is, combining terms with AND, OR and NOT?

Boolean searching enables the user to more closely specify the search. This is a traditional approach of commercial database services. In AltaVista Advanced Queries, Boolean is obligatory. Excite requires Boolean operators in upper case, for example `wizard` AND `oz`.

- Is Boolean syntax recognized, that is, grouping of search parameters with the use of parentheses, for example (`cricket` AND (`pitch` OR `ground`))?

Nesting of search terms allows for further fine tuning of searching. This is available with AltaVista.

- Can Boolean searching be combined with operators such as NEAR, FOLLOWED BY?

This can enable close specifying of the search. See for instance the options in OpenText's Power Search.

- Can you search for a phrase?

Commonly, the syntax for phrase searching, where it is provided for, is to enclose the phrase in inverted commas, for example "`formula one`". Phrase searching is offered by Infoseek Ultra, AltaVista and OpenText.

- Can the user indicate which search terms are a high priority?

Words that must be in the document can often by indicated with a plus sign, a facility offered by Infoseek, AltaVista, Infoseek and Excite. Another example is Excite's '^' which makes it possible to indicate which search terms are more crucial than others. Documents containing a given term can sometimes be excluded by using a minus sign as in Infoseek, AltaVista and Lycos.

- Are words treated as words, substrings, stems?
  - Does the search engine automatically truncate words? For example, a search for `anthropologist` is interpreted as a search for `anthropolog`.

  Lycos searches on the stem of the word unless a period (.) is given to indicate than an exact match is required, for example "`anthropologist.`"

  - Can you search by the word stem? For example, `anthropolog*` to cover `anthropology`, `anthropological`, `anthropologist`, and so on.

  Lycos uses a dollar sign to search on a word stem, for example `anthropolog$`.

  - Is case-sensitive searching provided for?

  Some search services interpret adjacent search terms starting with capital letters as proper names, for example Infoseek and Excite.

Flexibility in searching

- Can a search be restricted to specific data components (fields), for example hosts, applets, links?

Infoseek Ultra provides a Field Search option, for instance restricting the search to titles, sites, URLs or embedded hypertext links. Similarly AltaVista allows constrained searches.

- Can the search be limited by date, in particular, for looking for recent material only?

For example, AltaVista's Advanced Search provides for a Start Date and End Date limit on a search.

- If you find something useful, is there the facility to search for more of the same?

For example, Excite's More Like This link with each entry.

Valid assessment of relevance

- Does the list of matches rank first those documents in which all the search terms were found, or is the ranking based on a raw score of occurrences of any search words in the document?
- Does the position of search terms in the document count? Frequently it is a significant factor.
- Are less common words (in the language) given a higher relevance score?

Other factors which influence the ranking of search results

- Does the service sell keywords (selling of a guarantee of being found in the top ten hits for searches on a specified keyword)?
- Does the service protect itself from **index-spamming**?
- Are more commonly referenced pages listed first (using an analysis of links from other pages)?
- Can the user specify any criteria for ranking, for example location, date?

Informative presentation of results

- Are you given a total for matches found?

Many search engines provide this feature.

- What is included in the entry for each match? For example, title, part of text, URL, meta information such as keywords and description, size, date.

Most search engines take some portion of the text to provide an abstract. In each entry in its list of search results, AltaVista includes the date that the item was indexed.

- Are duplicates eliminated?

Infoseek Ultra claims to eliminate duplicates.

- Are the search results actual working links?

3.1.2 AltaVista

AltaVista (see Plate 2), made publicly available by Digital Equipment Corporation in December 1995, is an index searcher offering fast and flexible searching of a very large Web and Usenet News database.

Access

```
http://altavista.digital.com/
```

A European mirror site in Sweden offering access to AltaVista in over a dozen European languages is available from:

```
http://www.altavista.telia.com/
```

Coverage

AltaVista offers full-text indexing of some tens of millions of WWW documents as well as recent postings (a few weeks) to thousands of Usenet News newsgroups.

The AltaVista index is updated daily with new material. Existing entries are revisited according to the frequency at which they appear to change. Manually submitted URLs are added in on a daily basis.

Using

AltaVista offers *Simple* or *Advanced* Searches.

In response to a search, a list of matched items ranked in order of relevance is returned. Relevance of a document is determined by:

- how many of the search terms it contains;
- where the words are in the document (ranked higher if in first few words);
- how close to each other they are.

AltaVista usually gives a large number of hits unless the query is very specific.

Simple searching
AltaVista finds documents containing as many of the search terms as possible ranked so that documents with the most matches come first in the list of hits.

Advanced searching

Complex queries can be constructed within AltaVista's Advanced Searching option. For combining search words and phrases in the one search, the (Boolean) operators AND, OR, NEAR or NOT need to be used. Phrases are indicated with the use of quotes, for example `"nuclear diffusion reactor"`. Nesting of search terms is possible using parentheses (see Examples below). Searching on a word stem is possible, for example `librar*`.

It is possible to constrain searches to look for specific types of information (largely corresponding to HTML tags) such as applets, hosts, images or links.

Display

Entries can be displayed in compact, standard or detailed form. The standard entry includes the title, URL, description, size and date.

Interfaces

AltaVista offers interfaces to its database in over a dozen European languages. Search results are displayed in their original language. Text-Only interface is available.

Examples

Suppose that the search was for information about programmes for the training of a guide dog (or dogs) for the blind.

A Simple Search on the terms:

```
guide dog blind training school
```

gave six relevant hits on the first page, but included a few for '`blind dog`' right at the top of the list. In order to improve on the search, Advanced Search was used to look for:

```
"guide dog*" near blind and (training or school)
ranked by: "guide dog*" and (training or school)
```

This whittled down the hits from 10 000 to 400. Excepting one, all of the hits in the first ten were relevant to the search.

Finding more information

AltaVista provides a detailed Help file for both Simple and Advanced Queries. The AltaVista home page also provides a link to the document *Frequently Asked Questions about AltaVista*.

3.1.3 Excite

Excite is a full text Web searcher designed for natural language searching. Its concept-based architecture aims to support searching, browsing and exploration of the Internet. It claims to have the largest database of any of the Web search tools. One of its advanced features is the use of statistical techniques in the assessment of relevance, that is, it looks not just at the number of times that words occur in documents, but also at where they occur relative to one another and their position in the document.

Access

`http://www.excite.com/`

Coverage

Excite is a full text searcher of tens of millions of Web pages, thousands of newsgroups and a database of tens of thousand of Web site reviews.

The database is updated weekly.

Using

A notable feature of Excite's service is its concept-based searching. As well as searching for the exact words specified in the query, Excite expands the search to look for closely linked words. Its Help document cites this example:

> Suppose you enter *elderly people financial concerns* in the query box. In addition to finding sites containing those exact words, the spider will find sites mentioning the economic status of retired people and the financial concerns of senior citizens.

A simple search can be expressed in normal language, for example `training or schools for guide dogs for the blind`. However, more complex search requirements can also be accommodated with the use of keywords combined with Boolean operators and syntax, plus some other features. Boolean operators such as AND, OR, NOT must be expressed in upper case. Combinations of search terms can be grouped using parenthesis, for example

```
(schools OR training) AND guide AND dogs AND blind
```

Additional search features

If some search terms are more crucial than others, the user can indicate this by adding a ^ symbol at the end of a word. When searching for names, typing them in with a capital first letter will enable Excite to recognize them as names and search for documents where the terms are next to each other, for example `Jane Austen`.

If the information sought must have certain words in it, this can be specified in the search with a plus sign in front of the search word. Similarly, a minus sign in front of a word can exclude all documents containing this word.

Excite Search claims that its proprietary search technology, **Intelligent Concept Extraction**, finds more relevant documents than conventional search engines.

Display

In response to a search Excite reports on the number of documents found and lists hits ten at a time. Results include an automatically generated summary.

A sample entry from a list of matches of a search for *Guide to Network Resource Tools* follows:

```
100% Guide to Network Resource Tools (GNRT) [More Like This]
URL: http://www.terena.nl/libr/gnrt.html
Summary: The Guide to Network Resource Tools is in reconstruction. The
original EARN GNRT (1993-1994) is still available but considerably
outdated in some areas.
```

The entry shows that the Excite search engine has given this entry a 100% confidence rating. This rating determines the order in which search results are listed, unless a user requests that matches are listed by Web site.

Excite provides relevance matching through its [More Like This] link. Selecting this link generates a list of items similar to that resource.

Example

The search was on:

```
guide dogs for the blind training programmes or schools
```

Of the 1 284 607 documents Excite found, seven of the first ten were relevant to the search, and all were ranked by Excite as being above 90% relevance. The first ranked result was:

```
95% Guide Dogs [More Like This]
URL: http://laika.ed.csuohio.edu/empire/guide.dog.html
Summary: Guide dogs get to go with their masters and the dogs wear a
harness because they won't get away and they will lead the master
around. People at dog training schools train dogs to be a guide dog
```

Finding more information

Information on Excite can be found by selecting the Help link from its home page:

```
http://www.excite.com/Info/searching.html
```

This document provides search tips as well as instructions on advanced searching and on understanding your search results.

Some information about its spider program is available at

```
http://corp.excite.com/spider.html
```

3.1.4 Infoseek

Infoseek comprises two services, Ultrasmart and Ultraseek. Both services use the Ultra technology and both offer the choice of searching the Web, current news stories, email addresses, company profiles or Web FAQs. Ultrasmart aims to combine the dual approaches of searching and browsing, while Ultraseek is a search engine only.

Ultraseek concentrates on providing fast and flexible searching of a very large database. It uses a fast search engine with intelligent features for improving the accuracy and effectiveness of searching. Ultraseek claims to be able to perform 1000 queries per second on its database of tens of millions of documents.

Access

```
http://www.infoseek.com/
```

Coverage

Ultraseek includes an enormous index comprising some tens of millions of unique URLs, of which the majority are full-text indexed. The integrity of the database is supported by a process of elimination of dead links and duplicate pages and its currency is maintained by real-time indexing. Infoseek seeks to align its frequency of re-indexing of Web sites with the frequency at which pages change.

Using

Ultrasmart provides for natural language searching and integrates search results with related topics in its directory listing, and also offers links to news and other relevant services. In supplementing the search facility with a browsing option, it aims to provide for users who do not know precisely what they are looking for. These (and other) users are further supported by the facility for progressive refinement of the search by using the Search Only These Results option at the bottom of the page of search results.

Ultraseek is more of a service for power users, offering additional options for searching and also a larger database, but no links to browsable sources such as the directory listings. Natural language searching is possible but special search expressions are also allowed. It incorporates automatic proper name and phrase recognition.

Any search words or phrases can be given. Phrases may be indicated by quotation marks, for example

```
"guide dogs"
```

Required search terms can be denoted with a plus sign, and terms to be rejected with a minus sign, for example

```
"guide dogs" +blind -deaf
```

Infoseek attempts to intelligently interpret search terms. For instance it automatically recognizes proper names and phrases. It will extend a search to cover variant forms of a given word, for example

```
CDROM, CD-ROM, CD ROM
```

Using Ultraseek's field syntax, it is possible to confine the search to URLs, sites, titles or hypertext links. For example, to search for sites which include links to the TERENA Web server, the search terms would be:

```
link:http://www.terena.nl/
```

Display

Infoseek Ultra provides a report on the search, giving a document count for each search term plus a grand total. Results are ranked by relevance score. Each entry gives a hyperlinked title and optional summary consisting of a short text extract, URL and file size.

Example

Using Infoseek Ultra, a search for information about training or schools for guide dogs for the blind was carried out using the search terms:

```
training school +"guide dogs" for the blind
```

Any useful hits are likely to contain the phrase 'guide dogs', so this phrase is given a '+', indicating that only documents containing it are of interest. 1607 hits were found, three of which were assessed at 100% relevance (though in fact one of these was irrelevant). Nine of the first ten were primarily about guide dogs and included a couple of listings of schools for guide dogs. The lowest relevance percentage amongst the first ten was assessed by Infoseek at 97%.

Finding more information

Infoseek Ultra includes extensive information on its search engine and also help on searching.

3.1.5 Lycos

The Lycos search engine provides searching of a large robot-generated database. It offers a complementary Sites by Subject service which provides a classified hierarchy of subject resource lists.

Access

`http://www.lycos.com/`

Coverage

The Lycos database indexes some tens of millions of Web pages. (The total is given at the beginning of a page of search results.) It has a large number of binary files in its database including picture and movie files. It indexes ftp and gopher servers as well as Web sites.

Using

Lycos Search provides simple and advanced (Custom Search) searching. Both offer the option of searching:

- All sites – this option displays complete WWW search results.
- Pictures – displays GIF, JPEG and MOV files which match the query.
- Sounds – displays WAV, SND, RA and AU files which match the query.
- By subject – this searches in Lycos's Sites by Subject directory listing.

Multiple search terms are treated as if they had OR between them unless joining with AND is specified in Custom Search or the user selects the Match all Words radio button at the bottom of the search results window. Further options are available in Custom Search, notably the specifying of the number of search terms to be matched, for example in a search for `training guide dogs blind school` only four out of five are needed because `school` in this context is synonymous with `training`.

In Custom Search the user can specify a required level for goodness of match, that is, loose, fair, good, close or strong. This option effectively enables the user to specify a minimum relevance score which is acceptable. For example, a loose match will retrieve anything with a score of at least 10%, a fair match anything of at least 30%, right up to a strong match which equates to a score of 90% and higher. It is interesting to note that the Simple Search appears to have a default minimum requirement of 90% built in.

Display

Search results are prefaced with a statement of the number of matching documents found from Lycos's current total of indexed pages, as well as the terms it searched for, for example

```
You found 3 relevant documents from a total of 68,173,788 indexed Web
pages: guide , guided , guidelines , guides , dogs , blind , ...
```

Only one level of display is available. The list of matches gives for each entry the title, a short abstract taken from the start of the document, the URL, file size, the relevance score (percentage) and the number of terms matched, for example

```
1) Freedom Guide Dog Page
Freedom Guide Dog Page Freedom Guide Dogs Kingston NY Puppy Raisers
Homepage Puppy Raisers Needed for the Local Area!!!!!! Freedom Guide
Dogs for the ...
http://www1.mhv.net/~copyman101/welcome.htm (3k)
[100%, 3 of 3 terms relevant]
```

Lycos is a heavily used service and response times can be very slow.

Example

A simple search for

```
guide dog blind training school
```

returned 31 885 relevant documents with any of the terms matched, but even the highest ranked matched only three of the five terms. Only three of the first ten hits were about `guide dogs` while others concerned `training guides`, and a `guide training school` and `dog training`.

Custom Search did not improve on these results.

Finding more information

Very little information is provided on the Lycos site about the search engine. There is only a brief list of tips on searching.

3.1.6 OpenText Index

OpenText Index is a very large index searcher with some sophisticated search options.

Access

`http://www.opentext.net/`

Coverage

OpenText searches and indexes the full text of Web pages. It claims the largest index of all the search services currently. The updating process is continuous with over 50 000 Web pages added and updated per day.

Using

OpenText offers searching of its database for:

- a single word or group of words,
- a phrase,
- a combination of words and phrases,
- terms linked with operators `and`, `or`, `but not`, `near`, `followed by`,
- terms occurring in specific areas of the document, such as in the URL, title, heading or summary.

The initial choice of search is either *Simple Search* or *Power Search*. Simple Search enables you to search for a word or phrase. Power Search does this and more. It also offers searching of specific areas of a document. Up to three search terms can be specified in this way, and these terms may be combined with the operators listed above.

With its optional link Improve your Result on each search results page, OpenText offers a facility for progressive refinement of the search. Each selection of Improve your Result offers an additional field for input of search terms, plus a choice of Boolean operators. In this way vast hit lists can be whittled down to a well-focused and manageable list of references.

Results
The order of results is based on the number of times that the search term occurs in the document, as well as its position. For instance if it appears in the URL, this will be given a higher ranking than an occurrence in the body of the document. The summary is a combination of the title, first heading and some of the text.

Example

An advanced search was selected and the following search input:

```
guide dogs within anywhere
AND blind within anywhere
AND training within anywhere
```

There were 31 search results, but only a few of the top ranked ones were relevant to the search.

Finding more information

Search Tips and Help are available. There is also an FAQ.

3.2 Meta-search services

3.2.1 What are they?

Meta-search services (or meta-searchers) offer simultaneous searching of a number of search engines from one starting point. When the user keys in some search terms, the meta-searcher runs the search request on its associated search engines, and collects the results. It may then select from the results, process them and generate a composite list of hits, representing, in theory, the best matches from a range of search engines. It may then carry out some further processing of the results, for example allocating an overall relevance score, sorting by relevance or other criteria, formatting in a consistent manner, verifying availability and removing redundant URLs. The final list of results will be a collective list which usually indicates which search engine generated which entries. Possibly it might be grouped according to the originating search engine.

3.2.2 Pros and cons

In a situation where there are many different search engines to choose from, none of which is either perfect or comprehensive, and where the use of multiple approaches and tools to find information is a frequently recommended strategy, meta-search services would appear to hold out the promise of the ideal all-purpose solution. They have developed sophisticated searching and processing operations in order to monitor the performance and results of multiple simultaneous searches. But the task of generating and post-processing searches from a number of search engines and returning results within an acceptable time is an ambitious undertaking. So much relies on the effectiveness and speed of services over which there is no direct control, so it is not surprising that there are some trade-offs.

Coverage

The meta-searches need to deal in manageable quantities of information, so there are built-in cut-off points on search results. The result can be a surprisingly brief list of results.

Quality

The quality of the results ultimately relies on the indexing and searching capabilities of the search engines used. If even one of them generates rubbish, it will degrade the quality of the meta-searcher's results.

Control

Search engines use different search algorithms, and with a generic request there is not the same potential for close specification of the search, nor for further refinement.

Speed

If results are being presented as one integrated list, one slow search engine can impose delays on the display of all results.

The meta-searchers have looked for ways around these problems. For instance MetaCrawler incorporates a mechanism for verifying that items in the collective list of search results are actually accessible and are relevant to the search before displaying them. In selecting which search engines to use for a search, SavvySearch takes into account the current turn-around time for each search engine and gives preference to those which are faster.

3.2.3 MetaCrawler

MetaCrawler is a Web search service which searches several Web search engines simultaneously. It is a search engine of search engines.

Access

`http://www.metacrawler.com/`

Coverage

MetaCrawler has no database of its own but relies on the databases of the sources it uses, for example Lycos, WebCrawler, Excite, AltaVista, Yahoo, HotBot and Galaxy.

Using

MetaCrawler provides a single search window from which a search on multiple search engines is generated. In keying in search terms, users can specify whether they want hits which include any of the search terms, all of them or to have the search terms treated as a phrase. There is also a choice between a fast search and a comprehensive search.

MetaCrawler collates the search results into a single uniformly formatted list, eliminating duplicate URLs and verifying that the items in the list are accessible and relevant to the search. By default, search results are listed in order of relevance, with the confidence score given to each reference by the originating search engines taken into account in the ranking. A useful alternative, where geography is a factor, is the option of ranking results by location (sorted by top-level domain).

The additional option of the Java-enabled search control lets you see which search engines are being searched and how the search is progressing.

Example

A comprehensive phrase search for '`guide dogs for the blind`' found 43 hits, ranked by relevance, and generated by a number of search engines. Where a hit was duplicated, a composite entry was given, though not in all cases. Over half appeared to be directly relevant to the search terms.

Finding more information

The link on About from the home page answers some basic questions about MetaCrawler, albeit quite briefly.

3.2.4 SavvySearch

SavvySearch is a meta-search tool, which provides for simultaneous querying of multiple Internet search engines.

Access

`http://www.cs.colostate.edu/~dreiling/smartform.html`

Coverage

SavvySearch has no database of its own but offers a one-stop interface for querying multiple databases including Excite, Lycos, Yahoo, WebCrawler, Galaxy, DejaNews, Infoseek and Magellan.

Using

SavvySearch's query page invites you to select the type of information you are looking for, for example WWW Resources, People, Commercial, Technical Reports, Software, and so on and offers a choice of looking for all or any of the terms, or for documents in which the terms are next or near to each other. There are also options related to search results, such as how many hits and how much detail on them are required. Hits are grouped by the search service which generated them, though an option of integrating results, which removes duplicates, can be selected.

When a query is submitted, SavvySearch assesses which search engines will provide the best performance in satisfying it. Initially it uses just a small number (between two and five) of search engines for the search. The Search Plan (at the bottom of a list of search results) shows the ranking of search engines used and provides an option of selecting a further group of search tools for rerunning the search.

SavvySearch's query page is available in a range of languages.

Example

A search on the search terms '`training guide dogs blind`' gave results from Yahoo (1) and Excite (9), all of which were relevant.

Finding more information

There are links from the SavvySearch pages to a Help document and the FAQ. These provide adequate information on using the service.

3.3 Subject directories

Classing resources by subject provides an intelligently ordered view of a selection of Internet resources. Most important, listings organized in this way enable users to **browse** through hierarchical arrangements of resources, in the knowledge that some human intelligence, rather than a computer program, has been involved. This may be not so much a guarantee of the quality of any individual item, for in the case of many of these directories, submission of items for inclusion is open to anyone, but more a demonstration of the benefit of grouping like with like.

In looking for the appropriate tool for a search, it may be useful to note that subject-organized directories have the following features:

- **Context-based searching** As in a library arranged by subject, items are arranged with like items, and lateral browsing may offer fruitful possibilities.
- **Selected resources** Selectivity may well compensate for lack of comprehensiveness in some cases, for instance, in searching for a standard or classic work in a subject area.
- **Improved chance of finding quality resources** Even though many items may be self-selected by their authors, many will also have been selected for inclusion because they have been found useful by others.

- **Low risk of duplication and redundancy** In contrast to automatic index searching, selective human-compiled lists will not normally throw up multiple hits for the same work.

3.3.1 Subject organization

The system of subject organization may be no system at all but the ad hoc creation of the authors such as with Yahoo (Section 3.3.4), or it may be a standard library classification scheme such as UDC (Universal Decimal Classification). Standard library classification schemes offer the benefits of greater consistency and widespread recognition and acceptance.

Added value

Subject directories are a useful complement to search engines, but frequently individual entries are lacking in detail, and may in fact be just a URL. Listings with annotations or descriptive entries provide more information about the resources listed and increase their potential for usefulness. Unlike the search engines, these entries are human-generated rather than machine-generated and may in some cases, such as Magellan (Section 3.3.3), also include an evaluation of quality based on established criteria. Entries may be formally structured and use a standard list of fields, much like a library catalogue entry.

Most directories incorporate a search facility which searches just their database of entries.

3.3.2 Subject gateways

Taking the work of information professionals in taming the Internet information jungle a step further are the services which bring subject expertise to bear on the selection, classification and description of resources. These services, **subject gateways**, select, classify and describe quality resources in a specified subject area. They effectively fill the role of information broker for information seekers in that subject. If successful, they can be relied on to identify useful quality online resources, and to be an important resource for anyone working in a field in which there is a significant mass of online source material. An example of a service which successfully fills this type of role is SOSIG, the Social Science Information Gateway (Section 3.3.5).

3.3.3 Magellan

Magellan is a browsable and searchable online guide to Internet resources. Its directory of rated and reviewed Internet sites includes individual entries for each site, complete with quality rating.

Access

`http://www.mckinley.com/`

Magellan has been translated into French and German.

Coverage

Magellan includes Web sites, ftp and gopher servers, newsgroups and telnet locations. New sites are continuously being rated and reviewed by the editorial staff and added to a substantial database of tens of thousands of entries. Sites are selected for review based on the usefulness and entertaining quality of their content. As well as its directory of reviewed sites, Magellan includes a large searchable database of millions of sites not yet reviewed.

Using

Magellan has an easy-to-use interface, providing users with the option of either browsing through the subject hierarchy or searching the databases. Whether navigating or searching, the alternative option is always available, as well as links to Help files.

Browsing

From the home page, there is a list of broad topics from where browsing can begin. Selecting one of these leads to further subdivisions of the topic and to lists of resources classed within that topic. Each resource listed offers a link to a review of that resource. Each review contains a standard list of fields covering language, content, keywords, audience and contact information, and most notably, the evaluation. The evaluation gives a one- to four-star quality rating based on such criteria as comprehensiveness, currency, organization and navigational ease, and the catch-all concept of 'Net Appeal'. Lists of resources in the directory are arranged according to evaluation, that is four-star sites appear first on the list.

Searching

Searches can be run on the database of rated and reviewed sites, 'Green Light' sites, or the entire database. ('Green Light' denotes sites which contain no material intended for 'mature' audiences.) The Magellan FAQ urges users to keep their searches simple. Just enter search terms in the Search text box and click on Search. There are a few additional options such as the use of the plus sign with terms which must be included, and the minus sign with terms which are to be excluded. Information on these options is available from the Options icon beside the search window.

When a search is run, it generates:

- a list of related topics in the Magellan subject hierarchy,
- the number of hits,
- the option to reduce the number of results to rated and reviewed sites (indicating how many hits this would be),
- the list of results ranked by relevancy. Each item in the list includes title, brief description, link to the site, URL, and if it has been reviewed by Magellan, the star rating and a link to the review.

Example

A search was run on the complete database for:

`guide dog blind training`

There were 31 077 results of which four of the first ten were relevant. With descriptive entries it was relatively easy to identify the useful hits but further attempts to heighten relevance such as using the plus sign with the terms `dog` and `blind` did not improve this proportion of relevant items.

Running the same search on rated and reviewed sites returned no results initially, but when the search terms `guide dog blind` and `train` were used, the search found one site for a Service Dogs mailing list under the subject groups `Health and Medicine: Disabilities` and `Daily Living: Disabilities`. This may serve as a reminder that search facilities which are an adjunct to the main function of providing a browsable directory may not be as sophisticated in the handling of search terms as some of the services which specialize in searching large databases, that is, some of the search engines proper. Nevertheless when found, the one item in the rated and reviewed sites was highly relevant and with a four-star rating, looked as if it might have been worthwhile.

Finding more information

The Help icon on every page takes you to the FAQ.

From the Search window there is also an Options link which gives you information about search options.

3.3.4 Yahoo

Yahoo is an extensive listing of Internet resources arranged by subject. At the top level there are 14 broad subject categories, from any of which the user can browse through the hierarchy of increasingly narrow subcategories, within which relevant resources are listed.

Access

```
http://www.yahoo.com/
```

There are European mirror sites for Yahoo in France, Germany and the UK.

Coverage

Yahoo lists many thousands of resources within its 14 main subject headings. Entries may consist of title only, or title and a brief description. Titles are dynamically linked to the resource itself. The basic service is supplemented with many other listings, for example Yahooligans! for Kids, Today's News, Stock Quotes and so on.

Using

Yahoo is primarily a browsing tool, but there is also a search facility on the Yahoo database, as well as on Usenet newsgroups and email addresses. Like other subject classified directories, one of its main advantages is that it puts resources in their subject context, and makes it easy to survey what's available on any listed topic. It incorporates a simple ratings system using an icon beside items considered to have good presentation/content for their respective topic area.

Browsing
Browsing usually begins by selecting one of the 14 broad topics at the top level, then proceeding down through the subject hierarchy to reach the desired topic. For example, a user might select the top level category of Business and Economy, then proceed to the next level where there are links to general works on the subject such as Directories and Indices, to sub-categories, and to any actual titles in this category. In the case of Business and Economy, topics such as Business Schools, Classifieds, Companies, are listed each with an indication of the number of items they contain, for example Business Schools (449). Selecting any one of these takes you down to the next level where there may be further categories and/or resources listed.

Searching
At any point in browsing through the subject hierarchy, there is a Search window at the top of the page from where you can search all of Yahoo or confine the search to the category you are in. Subject hierarchies can be very extensive and deep, so the Search facility is a necessary adjunct.

Unless the category search is specified, Yahoo searches on its entire database to find items that match search keywords. It searches in its subject categories, its database of Web sites, Net Events and Chat, and most Recent

News Articles. The search generates a summary of best matches from each of the four areas, or if there were no results, it generates an AltaVista search. In any case, a link to an AltaVista search for the same search terms is given at the bottom of the search results.

A search can be customized by selecting the link Options (beside the Search window). From here, there is the option of searching Yahoo, Usenet News (DejaNews) or Email addresses (Four11). Searches can be limited to the last day, week, month, year or three years. Search terms can be joined with AND or OR, and regarded as a substring or a complete word. There are further options available with Yahoo's New Search.

Example

A search for:

```
guide dog blind train
```

with terms treated as substrings and joined with AND found one match within the category:

```
Business and Economy:Companies:Animals:Dogs:Organizations
```

The single resource returned was relevant to the search. A browse in the relevant item in the subject hierarchy revealed that there were no more promising items there.

Finding more information

Help is available from `http://www.yahoo.com/docs/info/help.html` and there is also an FAQ. For information on New Search, select the link from the home page.

3.3.5 SOSIG

The Social Science Information Gateway (SOSIG) (see Plate 3) provides a quality-controlled listing of online resources in social sciences and related areas. Each resource listed is described and classified using a standard entry template.

Access

```
http://www.sosig.ac.uk/
```

Coverage

UK and world wide resources in social science and allied subjects are listed and described by SOSIG. The definition of 'social science' is notably broad, taking in subjects such as accountancy, geography and military science. SOSIG stresses the quality element in its selection of resources to the extent that only subjects for which there are quality resources available online appear on the top-level menu. Its menus point to over 2000 resources. Resources are collected from many different sources, including (initially) user submission, and subject experts advise on specific areas. Each resource is classified using the Universal Decimal Classification scheme.

Using

The main function of SOSIG is to enable users to locate useful online resources in the social sciences. Its core content is a brief but informative entry on each resource listed. Two approaches to finding information are possible. The user can browse through lists of resources arranged by subject category or search for specific terms in the database of entries. Within the subject-classed lists, each item has links to its descriptive entry as well as a link to the actual resource. Entries include title, description, keywords and URL, for example:

```
Title: BIRON
Description:
BIRON contains the bibliographic details of the ESRC Data Archive
catalogue of over 3000 datasets, including the General Household
Survey, Census of Great Britain and the Gallup Political Polls.
Keywords:
social science, social research, data archive, bibliographic data,
statistics, economics
Accessible by:
http://dawww.essex.ac.uk/biron.html
```

The basic search of the SOSIG database looks for entries which contain all search terms, but it is also possible to do Boolean searching (combining terms with AND, OR or NOT) and to specify case-sensitive searching. Under Extended Search Options, there are additional options such as checking whether you want searches on the stem of search terms (the default), or specifying a particular type of resource to search for, for example image, organization, software.

Whether searching or browsing, the interface is simple and easy to use.

Example

A search on

```
guide dog or blind
```

gave three hits; two were mailing lists and one an information server on services for blind people.

Finding more information

Help is available from a Help link on the Search page.

3.4 Directory services

Online directory services (White Pages) provide a means of searching for people and computers on the net. No directory service can claim to be comprehensive, but this section covers some of the tools commonly used for providing Internet directory services. Some of the tools are used mainly for local directories, while others such as X.500 and LDAP can be used globally. Though the net cast by these tools collectively catches the contact details of millions of people, there are still many people covered only by local directories which use tools other than those listed here.

For general guidelines on searching for people, see Section 1.2.3.

3.4.1 CSO

CSO is an abbreviation of CCSO which stands for Computing and Communications Services Office at the University of Illinois, Urbana-Champaign where it was developed. Many universities use CSO to make student and staff information (for example, phone numbers, email addresses) available online. While the data collected may vary from one organization to another, a CSO directory can usually be searched by name, email address, department, and so on.

Access

CSO directories are made available via a server (**Phonebook Server**). The server is accessed with a **ph** client, either standalone (for example, WinPH for 32-bit Windows), or built into a WWW or gopher gateway. Also the mail program Eudora includes a ph client. The client is configured by the user to access a specific CSO server to search for information.

CSO is normally used to provide a directory of a single organization only. It is therefore necessary for the user to know which organization or server to run a search on. The Internet Nomenclator pilot project (`http://ds.internic.net/nomen/introduction.html`) attempts to provide integrated searching of multiple CSO servers.

3.4.2 Finger

Finger is a utility that displays information about users on a specified host computer. It can be used in two ways:

(1) to ask for information about a user, such as their login name or whether they are currently logged on. You need to provide the domain name of the machine that the person uses;
(2) to find out who else is currently logged on to the same machine that you are logged on to.

Access

Though originating from the Unix world, finger clients have been developed for other platforms. On a Unix system, type `finger user@domain` where `domain` is the Internet domain name of the host computer. Finger must be running on the remote machine (that is, the machine used by the person you're interested in locating).

3.4.3 LDAP

LDAP (Lightweight Directory Access Protocol) was originally intended to give clients on desktop computers access to X.500 directories. It has many similarities to X.500. Like X.500 LDAP defines a global directory structure, including how the information in a directory is to be organized and also the protocol for accessing the information. Unlike X.500 it is simpler in concept and more easily implemented and it also supports TCP/IP.

In common with X.500 the LDAP information model is based on the entry, which contains information about some object (for example, a person). Entries may include a mix of information such as JPEG photographs, sounds, URLs and PGP keys. Directory entries are arranged in a hierarchical tree-like structure.

Access

Access is via the WWW (see the list of national LDAP servers and other Public Directory Interfaces at `http://www.dante.net/np/pdi.html`) or via a native LDAP client on a desktop machine (available from `http://www.umich.edu/~rsug/ldap/ldclients.html`). Netscape Communicator is LDAP-enabled.

A new feature is access via the Web using the LDAP URL format, for example `ldap://ldap.widgets.com/ou=production,o=widgets,c=nl?one` (this query filters down the directory tree to entries in the production department).

3.4.4 Netfind

Netfind is a simple Internet White Pages directory that can be searched using keywords such as domain name. Given the name of a user and the rough description of where the user works, Netfind attempts to locate information about that Internet user. Once the domain has been narrowed down, Netfind uses finger to track down the person's name.

Access

There is a Web interface to Netfind at `http://alabanza.com/kabacoff/Inter-Links/netfind.html` and a list of telnet-accessible Netfind servers at `http://alabanza.com/kabacoff/Inter-Links/search/netfind2.html` (login: `netfind`).

3.4.5 Whois

Whois is both a directory and a protocol. The Whois directory is a searchable database of information about networks, networking organizations, domains, sites and the contacts associated with them. It can be used in the following ways:

- to find information about networks, domains and hosts;
- to locate contact information (people) for networks and domains;
- when registering a domain name, to see if the name is already in use.

The main Whois database is maintained by the Internic's Registration Services. An organization that registers a domain name is automatically added to the Whois database.

Access

Whois can be accessed through a local Whois client, through an interactive telnet session, through email or through the Internic's Web-based form at `http://rs.internic.net/cgi-bin/whois`.

3.4.6 X.500

X.500 is a standard for distributed directory services. The standard encompasses both the structure of the X.500 database and also the protocol used in querying the database. X.500 can be used for different types of directories. Its most notable implementation is a global White Pages service containing in excess of a million names contributed to by X.500 servers in dozens of countries.

X.500 provides a hierarchical database structure (for example, country/organization/organizational unit/person). The database consists of entries (one per object) which may describe persons, network resources, organizations, and so on, each with its own set of attributes.

Access

X.500 is based on the client–server model. The user with an X.500 client (known in the X.500 world as a **Directory User Agent** or **DUA**) can query an X.500 server (**Directory System Agent** or **DSA**). The server maintains the local X.500 database, but it can also communicate with other X.500 servers. If a query cannot be answered locally it may be passed on automatically to other X.500 servers and the response passed back to the user. To the user, it appears that the entire directory is accessible from the local server. As well as queries, X.500 also supports data management functions (addition, modification and deletion of entries).

A list of Public Directory Interfaces to the Nameflow Paradise service (including WWW, gopher, telnet, LDAP server) is made available by Dante at `http://www.dante.net/np/pdi.html`. A UK Web gateway, the Worldwide Directory Service, is at: `http://www.cse.bris.ac.uk/comms/ccrjh/search-form-world.html`. In the USA, the Internic also provides a country listing for X.500 searching at `http://ds1.internic.net:8888/`.

Further information

X.500 Directory related information at `http://www.nexor.com/public/directory.html`

Internic's Whois page at `http://rs.internic.net/tools/whois.html`

Critical Angle's *LDAP World* at `http://www.critical-angle.com/ldapworld/survey.html`

LDAP Roadmap and FAQ at `http://www-leland.stanford.edu/group/networking/directory/x500ldapfaq.html`

3.5 Archie

Archie is a tool which indexes and searches distributed data such as holdings lists of Internet file archives and contents of WWW servers. Its best known application is in indexing anonymous ftp archives on the Internet. It was one of the earliest tools that offered a means of searching for specific items across hundreds of servers on the Internet. Now this database of file archives covers over a thousand servers and some millions of files and the Archie software has migrated from its university base to become a commercial product of Bunyip Information Systems. In its commercial phase, the software has been developed and enhanced, and is now marketed as a general database tool for distributed collections of data, including Web data. However, in the context of network resource tools, it is most important as the system which provides the Internet Archives database.

What is the Internet Archives database?

The Internet Archives database is an index of the contents listings of anonymous ftp archives on the Internet. Archie provides a means of automatically gathering the data from the servers which house the archives, organizing it, maintaining it and providing a search interface to it. Like other Internet tools, Archie operates on the client–server model. Archie servers cooperate to provide a distributed system of indexing in which each Archie gathers data in its own geographic region. The results are shared to effectively provide a large, searchable Archie index of Internet information, worldwide in scope.

Access

Users can search the Archie database either using the WWW, telnet, electronic mail or dedicated Archie client software installed on their desktop machine.

WWW access

For most users, the Web is likely to be the preferred route. It uses software which they are likely to have already installed, that is a Web browser, it can be queried interactively and it enables ready retrieval of files located through a search. Archie-Web servers make available a Web form in which users can specify their search term, plus additional parameters. The data is then processed by the Archie server, and a list of hyperlinked hits generated. Retrieval is a simple matter of selecting a hyperlink.

Bunyip makes available a standard query interface which many Archie servers use. Alternatively, there is the ArchiePlex interface. Both use CGI technology to pass the user's query to the database and to give back the search results to the user.

Telnet access

Telnet access provides a terminal-based means of querying the Archie database. It is made available by a number of Archie servers. When connecting to one of these servers, use the standard login `archie`. After a banner message the command prompt will appear. Archie provides its own set of commands for querying its database. First-time users should try the Help command to get started.

Email access

Email access to Archie is available through a number of email Archie servers. Users with only email connectivity to the Internet can send Archie commands in an email message to one of these server addresses. The query will be processed and the results sent back to the user via email.

Local client access
Local client software such as WS Archie for the PC or Anarchie for the Apple Mac offers a flexible means of querying the Archie database. Public domain Archie clients are available for Macintosh, MS-DOS, OS/2, VMS, NeXT, Unix and X-Windows. The clients are available from the Archie sites using anonymous ftp, and are in the directories `/pub/archie/clients` or `/archie/clients`, for example

```
ftp://ftp.bunyip.com/pub/archie/clients
```

Coverage

Currently, Archie tracks the contents of over 1500 anonymous ftp and WWW archive sites throughout the Internet, visiting individual sites at a claimed rate of twice per month. Sites visited hold approximately 6 million files.

Using

Archie is most useful where the exact name (or part thereof) of the desired file is already known. It will search the contents listings of anonymous ftp or WWW archives, treating search terms as exact names, substrings or regular expressions, as case sensitive or insensitive, according to your specification. Additional options for searching may be offered which enable you to specify the maximum number of hits desired, the domain or server on which you would like the search run, whether your search terms should be joined with AND or OR, and so on. The WWW version of Archie provides online Help. For information on using Archie via telnet, email and a local client see Section 3.5.2.

Accessing Archie via the WWW provides not only an easy to use interface, but also integrated file retrieval through hyperlinked search results. When using Archie via telnet, email and some local clients, Archie provides locations only. Retrieving the files needs to be carried out as a separate operation, usually via ftp.

Example

This example search was carried out on the Austrian Archie-WWW server at `http://archie.univie.ac.at:8001/`.

Using the default options of the simple Archie search, that is, **anonymous ftp** (search in anonymous ftp archives), **substring** (find search terms wherever they occur even where they are just part of a name) and **insensitive** (do not distinguish between upper case and lower case), a search for the Usenet newsreader software `free agent` was composed, selecting under Advanced Searching the search term operator AND so that only hits with both terms `free` and `agent` would be returned. The search gave the following results:

```
(1)ftp.tuwien.ac.at
1 /infosys/mail
drwxr-xr-x 512 06:03:00 29 May 1997 GMT free_agent

(2)ftp.fu-berlin.de
2 /pc/win3/tcp-ip/slip-ppp/clients
-rw-r--r-- 1451068 23:00:00 07 Oct 1994 GMT free_agent

(3)infoserv.cc.uni-augsburg.de
3 /pub/pc/windows/tcpip/news
-rw-r--r-- 192 04:23:00 04 Jun 1996 GMT free_agent

4 /pub/pc/dos/tcpip/news
-rw-r--r-- 55834 22:00:00 22 Sep 1994 GMT free_agent

5 /pub/pc/win31_only/tcpip/news
-rw-r--r-- 473071 22:00:00 09 May 1994 GMT free_agent

(6)ftp.rz.uni-wuerzburg.de
6 /pub/local/networking/win31/news
-rw-r--r-- 356434 11:17:00 13 Feb 1997 GMT free_agent
```

Selecting on number 1 linked to the ftp directory at the University of Technology, Vienna, from where versions of Free Agent for Windows 16-bit and 32-bit could be retrieved by selecting the desired file.

Finding more information

Bunyip Information Systems' pages on Archie: at `http://www.bunyip.com/products/archie/`.

3.5.1 Archie servers

European Archie servers accessible via the Web, telnet and email are shown in Tables 3.1 to 3.3.

3.5.2 Details of using Archie

Using telnet

You can use telnet to connect to an Archie server interactively (see Table 3.2). At the login: prompt enter `archie`. The login procedure leaves the user at the prompt `archie>` indicating that the server is ready for user requests.

Table 3.1 European Archie servers accessible via the Web.

Country	Address
Austria	http://archie.univie.ac.at:8001/
Croatia	http://ds5000.irb.hr/ap/form.html
Czech Republic	http://www.zcu.cz/services/archieplexform.html
Finland	http://www.funet.fi/funet/archie/archieplexform.html
France	http://archie.univ-rennes1.fr/
Germany	http://www.th-darmstadt.de/archie/archieplex.html
Hungary	http://www.carnet.hr/cgi-bin/cppri?CP_8859?ftp/archie.html
Latvia	http://www.lanet.lv/services/archieplex/doc/form.html
Netherlands	http://www.twi.tudelft.nl/Local/archieplex/doc/form.html
Poland	http://www.bot.astrouw.edu.pl/archie_servers.html
Portugal	http://s700.uminho.pt/CGI/archieplex/archieplexform.html
Slovakia	http://www.somi.sk/archie.html
Sweden	http://archie.luth.se/archie
Switzerland	http://cuiwww.unige.ch/archieplexform.html
Turkey	http://www.tubitak.gov.tr/archieplex/public-form.html
UK	http://sunsite.doc.ic.ac.uk/archieplexform.html

Table 3.2 European Archie servers accessible via telnet.

Country	Address	ip address
Austria	archie.univie.ac.at	131.130.1.23
Belgium	archie.belnet.be	193.190.198.2
Finland	archie.funet.fi	128.214.248.46
France	archie.cru.fr	129.20.254.2
Germany	archie.th-darmstadt.de	130.83.22.1
Israel	archie.ac.il	132.65.208.15
Italy	archie.unipi.it	131.114.21.15
Poland	archie.icm.edu.pl	148.81.209.5
Spain	archie.rediris.es	130.206.1.5
Sweden	archie.luth.se	130.240.12.23
Switzerland	archie.switch.ch	193.5.24.1
UK	archie.doc.ic.ac.uk	193.63.255.1

For better response time, a query should be directed to the closest server.

Table 3.3 Addresses for Archie via email.

Country	Address
Austria	archie@archie.univie.ac.at
Belgium	archie@archie.belnet.be
Finland	archie@archie.funet.fi
France	archie@archie.univ.rennes1.fr
Germany	archie@archie.th.darmstadt.de
Italy	archie@archie.unipi.it
Poland	archie@archie.icm.edu.pl
Sweden	archie@archie.luth.se
Spain	archie@archie.rediris.es
UK	archie@archie.doc.ic.ac.uk
UK	archie@archie.hensa.ac.uk

Archie servers respond to the commands listed below; the way they respond can be defined using the special command set, which changes the values of a set of variables described at the end of this section.

The following commands are available:

`exit`, `quit`, `bye` exits Archie.

`help <command-name>` invokes the on-line help. If a command-name is given, the help request is restricted to that command. Pressing the Return key exits from the online help.

`list <pattern>` provides a list of the ftp servers in the database and the time at which they were last updated. The result is a list of site names, with the site IP address and date of the last update in the database. The optional parameter limits the list to sites matching `pattern`: the command `list` with no `pattern` will list all sites in the database (more than 1000 sites!). For example, `list \.de$` will list all German sites.

`site(*) site-name` lists the directories and subdirectories held in the database from a particular site-name. The result may be very long.

`whatis string` searches the database of software package descriptions for `string`. The search is case insensitive.

`prog string | pattern`

`find(+) string | pattern` searches the database for `string` or `pattern`. Searches may be performed in a number of different ways specified in the variable `search`, which also determines whether the parameter is treated as a string or as a pattern. The search produces a list of ftp site addresses which contain filenames matching the pattern or containing the string, the size of the file, its last modification date and its directory path. The number of matches is limited by the `maxhits` variable. The list can be sorted in different ways, depending on the value of the `sortby` variable. By default, the variables `search`, `maxhits` and `sortby` are set to, respectively, exact match search on `string`, 1000 hits and unsorted resulting list. A search can be aborted by typing the keyboard interrupt character; the list produced at that point will be displayed.

`mail <email> <,email2...>` places the result of the last command in a mail message and dispatches specified email address(es). If no mail address is specified as a parameter, the result is sent to the address specified in the variable `mailto`.

`show <variable>` displays the value of the given variable. If issued with no argument, it displays all variables. The Archie variables are shown below with the details of the `set` command.

`set variable value` changes the value of the specified Archie variable. The variables specify how other Archie commands should operate.

Variables and values are:

`compress(+) compress-method` specifies the compression method (`none` or `compress`) to be used before mailing a result with the mail command. The default is none.

`encode(+) encode-method` specifies the encoding method (`none` or `uuencode`) to be used before mailing a result with the mail command. This variable is ignored if compress is not set. The default is none.

`mailto email <,email2 ...>` specifies the email address(es) to be used when the `mail` command is issued with no arguments.

`maxhits number` specifies the maximum number of matches `prog` will generate (within the range 0 to 1000). The default value is 1000.

`search search-value` determines the kind of search performed on the database by the command `prog string | pattern`. `search-values` are:

- `sub` a partial and case insensitive search is performed with `string` on the database, for example: `"is" will match "islington" and "this" and "poison"`
- `subcase` as above but the search is case sensitive, for example `"TeX" will match "LaTeX" but not "Latex"`
- `exact` the parameter of `prog` (`string`) must *exactly* match the string in the database (including case). The fastest search method of all, and the default.
- `regex` here `pattern` is used as a Unix regular expression to match filenames during the database search.
- `sortby sort-value` describes how to sort the result of `prog`. `sort-values` are:
  - `hostname` on the ftp site address in lexical order.
  - `time` by the modification date, most recent first.
  - `size` by the size of the files or directories in the list, largest first.
  - `filename` on file or directory name in lexical order.
  - `none` unsorted (default).

  Reverse sorts can be carried out by prepending `r` to the `sortby` value given (for example, `rhostname` instead of `hostname`).

`term terminal-type <number-of-rows <number-of-columns>>` tells the Archie server what type of terminal you are using, and optionally its size in rows and columns, for example `set term xterm 24 100`.

Using electronic mail (email)

The domain addresses of the Archie email servers are listed in Table 3.3 (for example, `archie@archie.doc.ic.ac.uk`).

The email interface to an Archie server recognizes a subset of the commands described in 'Using telnet' above. These are described below. An empty message, or a message containing no valid requests, is treated as a Help request.

Archie commands are sent in the body part of the mail message, but the 'Subject' line is processed as if it were part of the main body. Command lines begin in the first column; all lines that do not match a valid command are ignored.

`help` sends you the Help file. The `help` command is exclusive, so other commands in the same message are ignored.

`path return-address`

`set mailto(+) return-address` specifies a return email address different from that which is extracted from the message header. If you do not receive a reply from the Archie server within several hours, you might need to add a path command to your message request.

`list pattern <pattern2 ...>` requests a list of the sites in the database that match `pattern`, with the time at which they were last updated. The result is a list with site names, site IP addresses and the date of each site's last update in the database.

`site(*) site-name` lists the directories and subdirectories of `site-name` in the database.

`whatis string <string2 ...>` searches the descriptions of software packages for each `string`. The search is case insensitive.

`prog pattern <pattern2 ...>`

`find(+) pattern <pattern2>` uses `pattern` as a Unix regular expression to be matched when searching the database. If multiple `patterns` are placed on one line, the results will be mailed back in one message. If several lines are sent, each containing a `prog` command, then multiple messages will be returned, one for each `prog` line. Results are sorted by ftp site address in lexical order. If `pattern` contains spaces, it must be quoted with single (`'`) or double (") quotes. The search is case insensitive.

`compress(*)` causes the result of the current request to be `compressed` and `uuencoded`. When you receive the reply, you should run it through `uudecode`, to produce a .Z file. You can then run `uncompress` on the .Z file and get the result of your request.

`set compress(+) compress-method` specifies the compression method (`none` or `compress`) to be used before mailing the result of the current request. The default is none.

`set encode(+) encode-method` specifies the encoding method (`none` or `uuencode`) to be used before mailing the result of the current request. This variable is ignored if compress is not set. The default is none.
Note: `set compress compress` and `set encode uuencode` would produce the same result as the former `compress` command.

`quit` nothing past this point is interpreted. Useful if a signature is automatically appended to the end of your mail messages.

Description of *pattern*
A *pattern* is a specification of a character string, and may include characters which take a special meaning. The special meaning will be lost if '\' is put before the character. The special characters are:

- `.` (period) this is the wildcard character that replaces any single character, for example '`....`' will match any four-character string.
- `^` (caret) if '`^`' appears at the beginning of the pattern, then only strings which start with the substring following the '`^`' will match the pattern. If the substring occurs anywhere else in the string it does not match the pattern, for example `"^efghi"` will match `"efghi"` or `"efghijlk"` but not `"abcefghi"`.
- `$` (dollar) if '`$`' appears at the end of the pattern, then the searched string must end with the substring preceding the '`$`'. If the substring occurs anywhere else in the searched string, it is not considered to match, for example `"efghi$"` will match `"efghi"` or `"abcdefghi"` but not `"efghijkl"`.

Using a local client

A graphical interface (GUI) enables you to access the Archie functions by pressing mouse buttons in order to select menu options.

Archie clients written for use without a graphical user interface require you to type in the command `archie`, followed by one or more parameters. If you omit the parameters you are given a list of the possible parameters with a short description of each one. A description of the parameters is given below, where angle brackets (<>) indicate an optional parameter and a vertical bar (|) indicates a choice of parameters.

```
archie <-parameters> string | pattern
```

`o` specifies an output file name to store the results (not available with all clients).

`l` lists the result one match per line. This form is suitable for parsing by programs.

`t` sorts the result by date.

`m#` specifies maximum number of matches to return (# within the range 0 to 1000). The default value is 95.

`h archie-server` specifies which Archie server should be used; if this parameter is not given, then the query will be sent to the default Archie server, if one is defined.

`L` lists known servers and the current default server.

The following group of optional parameters determines the kind of search performed on the database. They are mutually exclusive.

`s` a match occurs if the file/directory name contains `string`. The search is case insensitive.

`c` as above, but the search is case sensitive.

`e` here `string` must *exactly* match (including case) the file/directory name in the database. This is the *default* search method.

`r` searches the database using `pattern`. It contains special characters which must be interpreted before performing the search.

There may be slight differences in the options available with different clients on different platforms.

The result is a list of ftp site addresses which contain files or directories matching the argument, together with the size of the file, its last modification date and its directory. By default, the list is sorted by host address.

3.6 Intelligent agents

Intelligent agents (software agents) are programs which carry out tasks on behalf of users. The spectrum of capability of agents is wide, ranging from the basic level of automating straightforward routine tasks through to the ability to adapt to user routines and preferences, and even to negotiate on behalf of users. The feature which distinguishes agents from other programs is the ability to automatically adapt their behaviour to the conditions they encounter and to make decisions based on a set of inbuilt rules and criteria, without specific on-the-spot instruction from the user. Agents may possess this feature of **autonomy** to a greater or lesser degree, depending on their sophistication. The capacity for autonomous behaviour may extend to taking the initiative, for example providing the user with information not specifically requested but likely to be of interest.

Agents may also communicate with one another and with other programs or people to obtain information or enlist help. Some are also capable of travelling between host computers (**mobile agents**).

In the area of Internet information searching, intelligent agents use their autonomy to add another dimension to traditional search facilities. For instance, they may decide how and where to search for a required piece of information, dynamically adapting their actions in response to the network environment as the search is carried out.

Access

An agent can be run on a client (the user's machine) or on a Web server (though mobile agents are not confined to a single location and may travel from client to server). There is a great deal of client-based agent software available on the net for a range of platforms (see 'Examples' below). Some is free, but many agent packages are commercial products available for purchase (such as WebCompass). Short-term trial versions of shareware packages (such as More Like This) may be available for free download.

Server-based agents (for example, Bargain Finder, Firefly) can be accessed via their URLs. Some of these online agents may require users to go through a registration process which gives them a re-usable logon and password.

Coverage

Agent software is used in a variety of contexts such as system administration, information searching on the Internet, current awareness services, online shopping, and so on. Some of the specific tasks which agents can be used for include:

- to enrich the user's net browsing by suggesting additional hyperlinks, based on previous user behaviour;
- to give added value to searches of conventional search engine databases such as AltaVista, Lycos, Infoseek, and so on;
- to run searches on multiple databases, filter and assemble the results in an intelligent way;
- to find the best price for a given product from online markets;
- to engage in transactions and negotiations on behalf of the user;
- to monitor databases on the WWW and provide a regular updating service;
- to monitor Web site changes;
- to compile a daily personalized newspaper;
- to visit sites nominated by the user and download either the entire site or selected pages for offline viewing;
- to discover other people with common interests;
- to check and prioritize email, make decisions based on content and act on them.

Using

Some agents come with their inbuilt sets of rules and criteria already in place, or their task is a circumscribed one. These require little or no configuration. Others need to be 'trained'. That is, they can be provided with sets of rules by the user. This may be a more time-consuming process, but in the end, will give a product tailor-made to individual requirements.

Examples

Autonomy Agentware `http://www.agentware.com/index.html` A suite of intelligent agent software which allows users to create their own personal intelligent agents on their PCs. As they are used, the agents continually learn more about the user's interests and adapt their behaviour accordingly. Autonomy's agents will perform such tasks as:

- searching the Internet to bring back information relevant to interests,
- compiling a personalized daily newspaper,
- managing email,
- censoring Web pages.

Bargain Finder `http://bf.cstar.ac.com/bf/` Gets the best price for CDs. Bargain Finder is an experiment in comparison shopping online, created by Andersen Consulting.

Firefly `http://www.agents-inc.com/` Server-based agent which takes input from users regarding their tastes and preferences in pop music and film, and outputs recommendations of titles which they might enjoy.

LiveAgent (AgentSoft) `http://www.agentsoft.com/liveagen.htm` A utility for creating personalized Java agents. The user goes through a regular Web browsing session. LiveAgent learns from this walk-through session and generates an agent that is capable of doing that activitiy by itself whenever the user wants.

More Like This `http://www.morelikethis.com` Takes the search terms given by the user, enriches and enhances them using a set of inbuilt rules, then searches the database of a selected search engine for relevant matches.

Search'97 (Verity) `http:/www.agents-inc.com` One of Verity's suite of products for retrieving, navigating and processing online information from the desktop. Search'97 offers a toolkit for building personal retrieval agents to proactively search, filter, categorize and deliver information to users from a variety of different sources. Works in conjunction with Verity's Search'97 information server information retrieval platform.

WebCompass (Quarterdeck) `http://arachnid.quarterdeck.com/qdeck/products/wc20` Travels to multiple search engines running the same search, then organizes and presents a descriptive list of results ranked by relevancy. WebCompass compiles an index of results and can be instructed to provide regular update information, for instance in the form of a daily electronic newspaper.

Finding more information

UMBC AgentWeb at `http://www.cs.umbc.edu/agents/`

@gency at `http://www.info.unicaen.fr/~serge/sma.html`

Sverker Janson: ***Intelligent Software Agents*** at `http://www.sics.se/isl/abc/survey.html`

The Agent Society at `http://www.agent.org/`

Computer Information Society at `http://www.compinfo.co.uk/`

Agent Sourcebook at `http://www.opensesame.com/agents/`

See also background articles in the Bibliography.

4 Group Communication

The most widespread means of group communication on the networks are the well-established tools, mailing lists and Usenet News. These provide a highly flexible and popular means of network communication for interest groups. A feature of their flexibility is that simultaneous connection between message sender and recipients isn't necessary. This type of communication is known as 'asychronous' communication. The complementary mode of 'synchronous' communication is employed by a whole swathe of tools which enable the people involved to connect simultaneously and communicate interactively with each other. These real-time communication tools come in a variety of media, ranging from plain text to full-blown multimedia. Collaboration tools employ both methods to facilitate the business of working together online.

This chapter covers the following tools:

- mailing lists, including LISTSERV,
- Usenet News,
- Web conferencing,
- real-time multimedia communication tools,
- collaboration tools, including client software and IRC (Internet Relay Chat).

4.1 Mailing lists

Email is an enormously flexible medium, one of its most versatile features being the ease with which one message can be sent to multiple recipients. This apparently simple feature is the foundation for the operation of mailing lists (or discussion lists) and the seedbed for the development of associated 'electronic communities'. Mailing lists enable people with a common interest to meet (virtually), exchange views, circulate news and announcements, make documents available to each other and pool their expertise to solve common problems. The discussion on a mailing list normally focuses on a single subject, though this subject may be a fairly broad one, encompassing many subtopics.

4.1.1 How do mailing lists work?

The facility for sending one message to multiple recipients is common to all email programs. Multiple email addresses can be grouped under one collective name, often referred to as an **alias** by the email program. This means that you can in fact have a sort of home-made mailing list from your local mail program, adding and removing addresses from the alias manually. There are also Unix utilities which will administer distribution lists. However, dedicated **mailing list manager** software running on a server offers the greatest functionality and capability for large-scale management of mailing lists. Most mailing lists on the networks are managed by one or other of several highly developed Mailing List Managers (MLMs), such as LISTSERV (see Section 4.1.7), Majordomo, Listproc and Mailbase. Mailing list manager software may provide some or all of the following functions:

- automated processing of subscriptions,
- distribution of messages,
- making available files associated with the list such as the monthly archives of messages,
- searching and indexing of message archives.

Refer to the *Mailing List Management Software FAQ* at `ftp://ftp.uu.net/usenet/news.answers/mail/list-admin/software-faq` for further information on MLMs.

Each mailing list will have a person responsible for the operation of the list. This is the **list owner**. The list owner will see that the list runs smoothly, provide any necessary information files, answer questions from members, and so on. Some lists are open to anyone. Others are **closed**, in which case the list owner will probably invite selected individuals to join the list and add them manually.

4.1.2 Locating a mailing list

There are thousands of mailing lists on a vast variety of topics. Refer to Section 1.2.1 for sources to search for mailing lists on a specific topic.

If you cannot find a list on the topic of your interest, you might look at setting up a list yourself. See the *List Owner's Manual for LISTSERV* at `http://www.lsoft.com/manuals/ownerindex.html` for guidelines on running a LISTSERV list. For UK academic users, there are documents on starting up and running a list from Mailbase at `http://www.mailbase.ac.uk/docs/owners-welcome.html`.

4.1.3 Joining a mailing list

Joining a mailing list is very simple. You send an email message containing a 'subscribe' or a 'join' command to the administrative address of the list. This usually looks something like this:

```
subscribe <listname> <YourFirstName> <YourLastName>
```

Substitute as appropriate between the angle brackets. Usually, you will then receive a message informing you that you are now subscribed to the list.

It is important to remember that the 'subscribe' message, and other administrative messages as well, should go to the administrative address, not to the list itself. With an automated mailing list, administrative messages are processed automatically by the MLM. If you send such messages to the list itself, they will normally be distributed to every subscriber to the list, which besides generating a certain amount of irritation, wastes everyone's time including your own, as your message won't have achieved the intended objective. Some mailing lists may have a moderator who weeds out unsuitable messages (such as 'subscribe') before they are distributed to the list, or possibly a smart MLM will reject such messages, but this cannot be assumed.

Here are some examples of administrative addresses:

```
LISTSERV@TERENA.NL
mailbase@mailbase.ac.uk
```

Here are examples of list addresses:

```
wg-isus@terena.nl
child-health@mailbase.ac.uk
```

4.1.4 Commands

MLMs respond to commands in email messages. Commonly, they will handle commands to:

- subscribe to a list,
- leave a list,
- receive a list in digest format,
- suspend mail temporarily,
- obtain a list of subscribers,
- obtain a list of archive files,
- search and retrieve archive files.

Consult the MLM's Help file (send email to administrative address with the text `help`) for information on their commands or see a comparative listing of MLM commands by James Milles of Saint Louis University Law Library at `http://lawlib.slu.edu/training/mailser.htm`.

4.1.5 Handling mailing list correspondence

Some lists are very active and generate a lot of messages each day. With others weeks may go by without any traffic. If you belong to a mailing list you need to learn to cope with the mail it generates. When there is a lot of incoming mail, you need to be discriminating about the email you read and the email you retain. The initial filtering of messages can be done by scanning the Subject field of messages and deleting those you recognize as not relevant to you. If your mail program has a filtering capability, you can configure it to sort (and delete) nominated categories of incoming mail. Whichever filtering process you use, you'll need to act decisively on the messages that remain. Decide which messages should be discarded, which acted upon, and which retained for reference, then follow up accordingly. Set up a logical filing system for retained messages. Later when you need the information, it's useful to be able to refer to all the correspondence on one particular subject.

Remember to make use of the facilities which the mailing list provides. For instance you may opt for a daily digest of messages (all the messages put together in one message), or suspend the list while you are on holiday. If the mailing list provides a browsable archive of messages, you can always refer to that to see what you have missed. In fact, with some busy mailing lists, regular scanning of the message archive for items of interest may be preferable to subscribing.

4.1.6 List etiquette

For guidelines on mailing list etiquette see Section 1.11 'Netiquette'.

4.1.7 LISTSERV

LISTSERV is a system for the creation, management and control of electronic mailing lists. It originated in the Bitnet network where it played an important role as a facilitator of networked scholarly communication for the research and education communities constituting Bitnet's user base. It is now the most widely deployed mailing list manager package on the networks and millions of LISTSERV list messages are sent each day.

LISTSERV lists are maintained by LISTSERV servers (**listservers**). For each list that it maintains, a listserver will manage the subscriber list, distribute list messages, make associated documents available, log mail traffic, archive messages and also carry out database searches of archives and files in response to email commands.

Access

LISTSERV is now commercial software available from L-Soft International and is available for VM, VMS, Unix (13 brands), Windows NT and

Windows 95. A free version, LISTSERV Lite, is available for small-scale non-profit mailing list management (up to ten mailing lists).

Anyone with access to email can join a public LISTSERV list. Simply send a subscribe message to the listserver, for example Send to:

```
LISTSERV@LISTSERV.ACSU.BUFFALO.EDU
```

the message

```
SUBSCRIBE NETTRAIN Mary Smith
```

With a public list, anyone can join or leave, send messages, see who is on the list, search the database, and so on. With private lists, you usually need to apply for membership to the list owner, and only people who are subscribed to the list may send messages and access archived postings.

LISTSERV is an email medium par excellence. Messages are sent to LISTSERV mailing lists by email, and all LISTSERV functions are accessed by email command, from straightforward `subscribe` and `unsubscribe` commands through to complex database searching functions. Remember that email commands go to the **LISTSERV server**, for example `LISTSERV@LISTSERV.ACSU.BUFFALO.EDU`, while messages to the list are sent to the **list address**, for example `NETTRAIN@LISTSERV.ACSU.BUFFALO.EDU`.

However, with the most recent versions of the LISTSERV software, it is possible to access some of LISTSERV's functions via the World Wide Web. Some LISTSERV lists may also be available via Usenet News through a gateway. Such newsgroups will come under the hierarchy `bit.listserv`. For instance NETTRAIN is available as a newsgroup titled `bit.listserv.nettrain`.

Coverage

LISTSERV lists are maintained by many servers and cover a vast range of topics. A distributed database of information about all publicly-accessible LISTSERV lists is automatically generated and maintained. To obtain a list of the lists it maintains, you can send an email containing the word `List` to any LISTSERV server. To obtain a list of LISTSERV lists dealing with a particular topic, you can make a keyword search of the global list of lists:

```
LIST GLOBAL <keyword>
```

The chances of finding something relevant are probably quite high given that there are currently more than 11 000 public lists. You can also search for lists via the WWW at the CataList Reference Web site maintained by L-Soft at `http://www.lsoft.com/lists/listref.html`. Here you can get a broad picture of the scale and variety of LISTSERV lists by browsing through lists of lists. You can also search for LISTSERV lists by topic, get details on each list, browse message archives and even subscribe.

Using

LISTSERV offers a great deal of functionality to support the administration of its mailing lists and to give users a range of options covering the way in which they receive list messages, files, information and request database searches. All of these functions can be accessed through email commands which are placed in the body of the message, for example

```
HELP
```

Email commands are addressed to a LISTSERV server and *never* to an actual list. If your commands relate to a particular list, it is preferable to send email commands to the specific LISTSERV server which manages that list if you know the address. Otherwise, the general LISTSERV address:

```
LISTSERV@LISTSERV.NET
```

may be used and your message will be forwarded to the correct server. This address can also be used for any information requests, such as Help or Info.

When a LISTSERV server receives an email command, it will ignore the 'Subject:' line of the mail header, so your commands must be in the body of the message. Several commands can be sent to LISTSERV in the same mail message, with each command on a separate line.

Some of LISTSERV's commonly used commands are listed in Tables 4.1 and 4.2.

Table 4.1 List participation.

Command	**Meaning**
`SUBSCRIBE <listname> <FirstName> <LastName>`	Join the list.
`SIGNOFF <listname>`	Leave the list. To sign off every LISTSERV list you are on, add a space and a * after the command
`SET <listname> DIGEST`	Receive the list in digest format, i.e. a day's or week's messages rolled into one
`SET <listname> NODIGEST`	Receive the list as separate messages, not in digest format
`SET <listname> NOMAIL`	Suspend mail temporarily
`SET <listname> MAIL`	Resume mail
`SET <listname> CONCEAL`	Do not display your address in the list of subscribers
`REGISTER <YourName>`	Tell LISTSERV about your name
`QUERY <listname>`	Query your personal list options, e.g. how you receive mail from the list

4.2 Obtaining information and files.

Command	Meaning
`REVIEW <listname> F=MAIL`	Send a list of subscribers. (F is the format requested. Other options include MIME/text, MIME/Appl, UUencode)
`LISTS`	Send a list of lists maintained by the server
`LIST GLOBAL <keyword>`	Send a list of LISTSERV lists (from any server) with this keyword in the description
`INDEX <listname>`	Send a list of archive files for this list
`GET <filename><filetype> <listname> F=MAIL`	Send this archive file

More detailed information on commands can be obtained by requesting LISTSERV command reference cards. For information on general user commands send this command to a LISTSERV server:

```
GET LISTSERV REFCARD
```

Joining lists

When you join a list, LISTSERV adds to its membership database information on your name and email address and assigns you a default set of list options unless you specify otherwise. The command `SET` enables you to change the options to suit yourself. There are additional options on most commands. You can find more detail on list commands and options in Section 4.1.8.

Obtaining files

Files can be stored at a LISTSERV server and made available for retrieval by users. There are two types of files stored:

(1) miscellaneous files relevant to the list deposited by the list owner or administrator;
(2) archives of email distributed to the list.

You can obtain a list of all the files associated with a list by sending to a LISTSERV server the email command:

```
INDEX <listname>
```

then follow up with an email request for specific files.

Archive files enable users to refer back to list mail distributed during a specific period. Commonly each month's messages will be stored in a separate log file. Past correspondence on the list can be accessed in two ways:

(1) Request a copy of the required log file.
(2) Use the database functions to search the archives for messages dealing with a particular topic.

Refer to 'Commands for files' in Section 4.1.8 for further information.

Database commands

The traditional medium for searching LISTSERV databases is by email command. Refer to 'LISTSERV database functions' in Section 4.1.8 for details of commands by email. Database searches can also be conducted via the World Wide Web if the list provides a WWW interface to its archive. You can see this demonstrated on the CataList Web site at `http://www.lsoft.com/lists/listref.html`.

Example

Suppose you wish to subscribe to the NETTRAIN list at `UVBM.BUFFALO.CC.EDU`. Your full name is Mark P. Waugh. Send the following command to `LISTSERV@UVBM.BUFFALO.CC.EDU`

```
SUBSCRIBE NETTRAIN Mark P. Waugh
```

Suppose you wish to leave the INFO-MAC mailing list (to which you have already subscribed) at the node CEARN. The command:

```
UNSUBSCRIBE INFO-MAC
```

should be sent to the LISTSERV server at CEARN which manages the INFO-MAC list. To leave all the LISTSERV lists you belong to throughout the network, send the following command to your nearest (or any) LISTSERV:

```
UNSUBSCRIBE * (NETWIDE
```

Suppose you wish to receive a listing of all mailing lists that have the text `europe` in their name or title. Send the following command to your nearest (or any) LISTSERV server:

```
LIST GLOBAL EUROPE
```

If you want to stop receiving mail from all the lists at SEARN to which you belong, send the following command to the LISTSERV server at SEARN:

```
SET * NOMAIL
```

Suppose you wish to retrieve the file `PCPROG ZIP` from a filelist, in `XXE` file format. Send the following command to the LISTSERV server that holds this file:

```
GET PCPROG ZIP F=XXE
```

Finding more information

LISTSERV provides a copious amount of information about itself and its functionality. A standard set of help files are available upon request from each LISTSERV server. You can obtain a list of these by sending the email command `INFO` to a LISTSERV server. To obtain a list of commonly used commands send an email message containing the word:

```
HELP
```

to:

```
LISTSERV@LISTSERV.NET
```

or to any LISTSERV server.

All of L-Soft's manuals for LISTSERV are available in ASCII-text format via LISTSERV and in popular word-processing formats via `ftp.lsoft.com`. They are also available on the World Wide Web at the following URL:

```
http://www.lsoft.com/manuals/index.html
```

Resources for list owners

CataList Web site at `http://www.lsoft.com/lists/listref.html` select Mailing Lists of Interest to List Owners.

LISTSERV List Owners Manual at `http://www.lsoft.com/manuals/ownerindex.html`.

4.1.8 LISTSERV commands

Commonly used commands are described here, including notes on optional parameters which may be used with them.

In the following descriptions, CAPITAL letters indicate acceptable abbreviations, angle brackets (<>) indicate an optional parameter and a vertical bar (|) indicates a choice of parameters. All parameters are fully explained in each command description.

A standard set of command keywords are available for use in some LISTSERV commands; they are shown in the command descriptions as optional parameters. The important standard keywords are:

`PW= password` You can register a personal password on a LISTSERV server, and thereafter you will have to validate certain commands by using the `PW=` command keyword in the command text. See the `PW` command for details on registering personal passwords.

`F= format` This keyword controls the file format (or internal file structure) in which files will be sent to you. Any user may specify a file format other than their default by using the `F=format` keyword in the commands where it appears as an option. The following file formats are valid for all users: `XXE`, `UUe`, `MIME/text`, `MIME/Appl`, `MAIL`.

Commands for lists

`SUBscribe list-name <full-name>` Use the `SUBscribe` command to join a mailing list, or to alter the name (but not email address) by which you are known on a mailing list you have already joined. The `list-name` parameter is the name of the list to which you want to subscribe. The optional `full-name` parameter allows you to give a name by which you want to be known on a mailing list. If specified, it should be your full, real name (at least your first name and last name) and not your email address.

Subscription to a list may be OPEN, CLOSED, or BY-OWNER. If it is OPEN, you will be automatically added to the list and sent notification. If it is CLOSED, you will not be added to the list, and LISTSERV will send you a message telling you that your request has been rejected. If it is BY-OWNER, your subscription request will be forwarded to the list owner(s), who will decide whether or not to add you to the list.

`UNSubscribe list-name | * <(NETWIDE>` Use the `UNSubscribe` command to leave a mailing list. The `list-name` parameter is the name (not the address) of a mailing list from which you want to remove your subscription. You can sign off all the lists to which you are a member at any particular LISTSERV site by using the '`*`' (asterisk) character instead of a list name. If you want your `UNSubscribe` command to be propagated to all LISTSERV servers on the network, include the `(NETWIDE` option. Use this option if you are changing your email address or are leaving your computer for an extended period.

`List <options> <F= format>` Use this command to get a listing of available mailing lists at a LISTSERV server. The important options are:

> `Short` This is the default; it displays a summary of all the lists managed by a LISTSERV in a brief, one-line description.
>
> `Long` The `Long` (or `Detailed`) option will send you a file called `node-name LISTS`, containing a comprehensive description of the lists managed by a LISTSERV server.
>
> `Global <pattern>` This option gives a complete list of all known LISTSERV mailing lists at all servers at the time the command is issued. The optional `pattern` parameter can be used to match any string in the list name, list title or list address.

`REView list-name <(> <options>` Use this command to receive information about a mailing list, including list control information and a list of subscribers. Note that at the discretion of the list owner(s), viewing of the list of subscribers can be restricted to list members only. The important options are:

> `Short` This option restricts the information you receive to the control section of a list (giving its definition parameters).

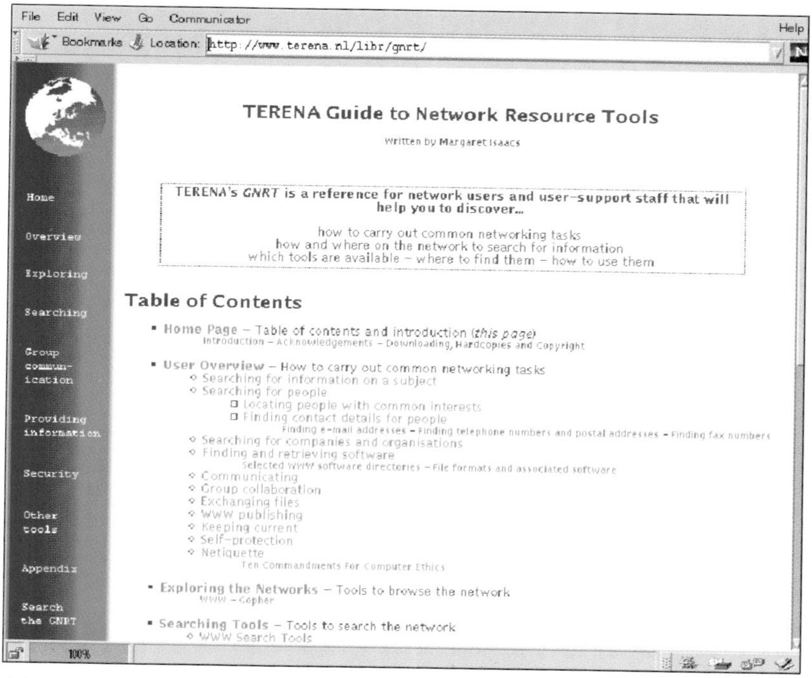

Plate 1 The online version of the guide

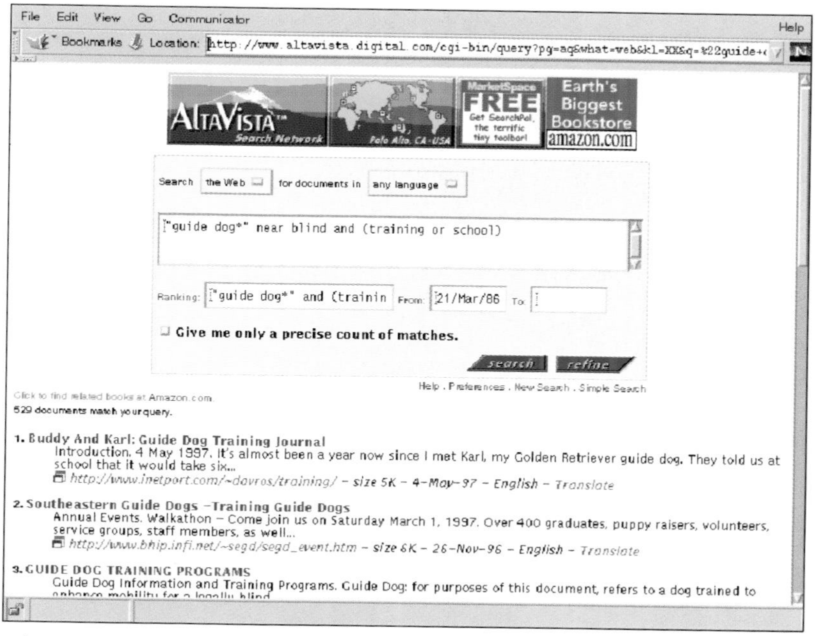

Plate 2 AltaVista's web search tool

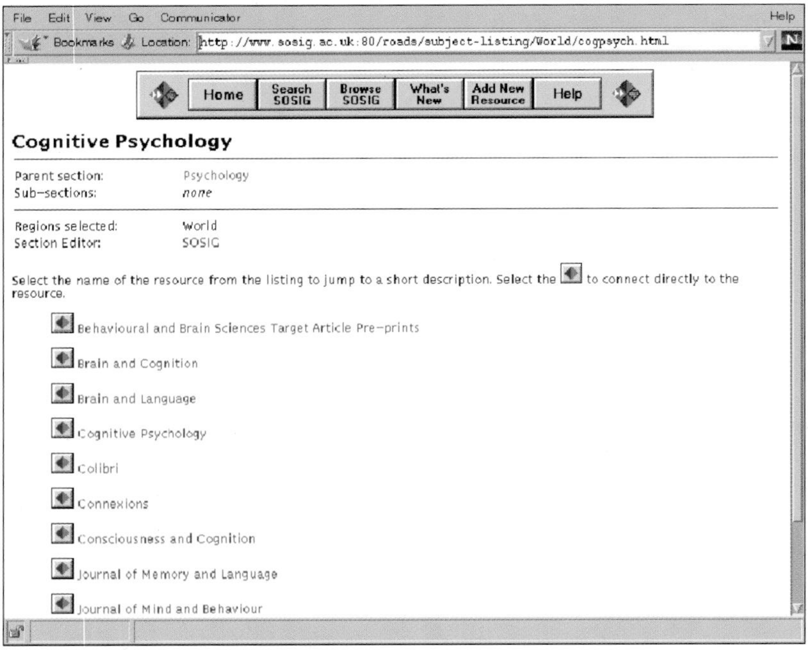

Plate 3 The Social Science Information Gateway (SOSIG)

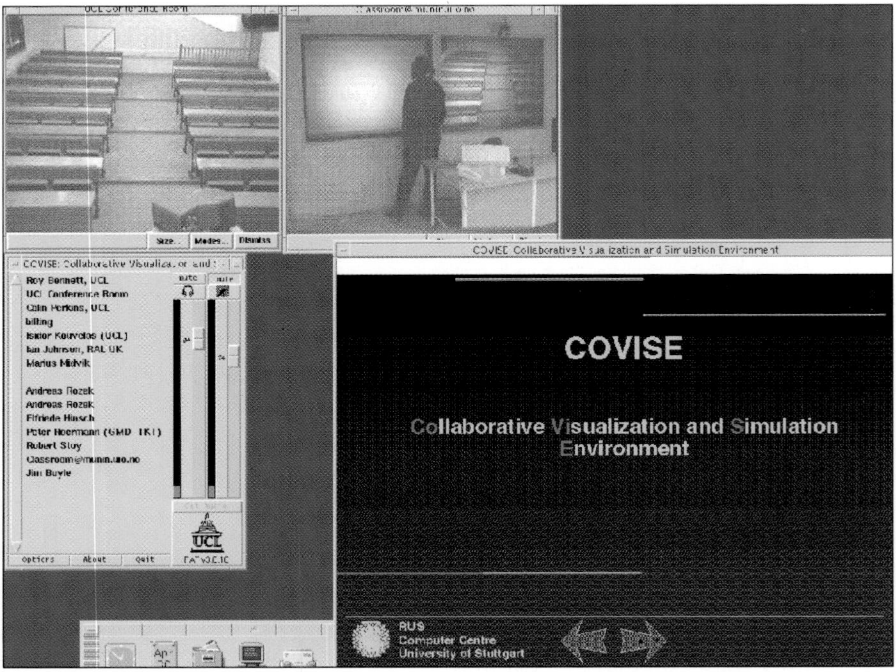

Plate 4 MBone videoconferencing tools

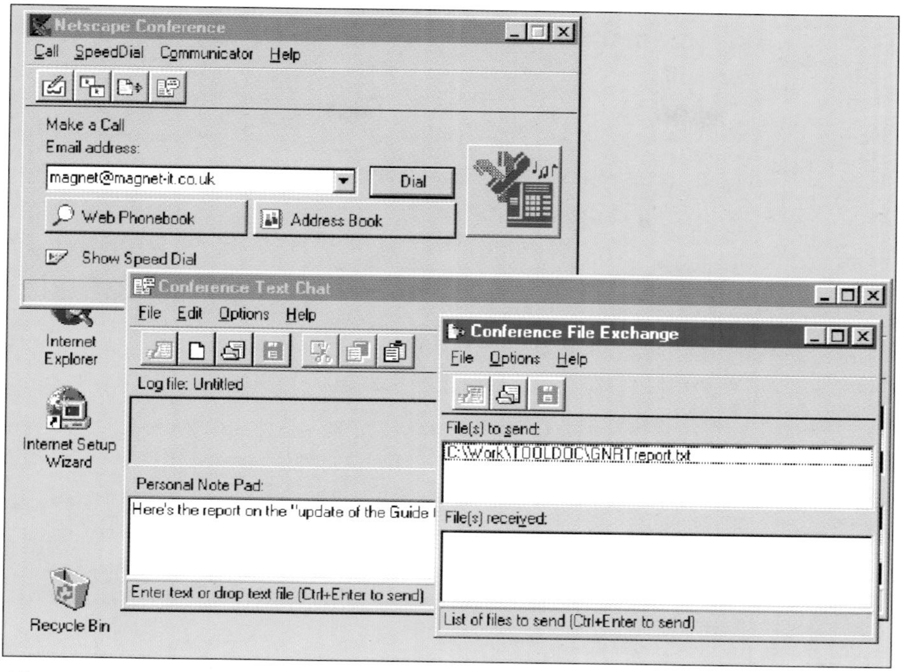

Plate 5 Netscape Conference

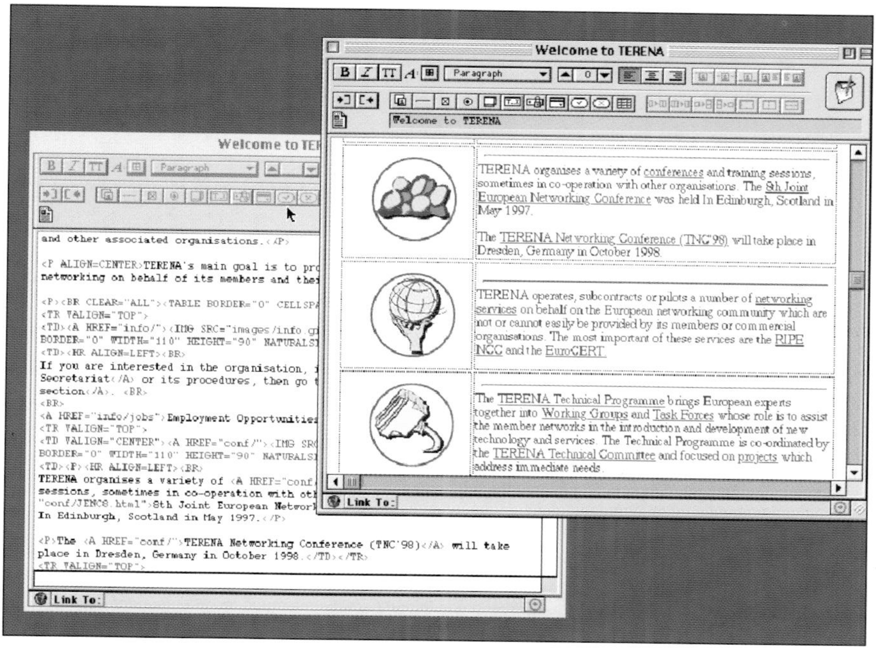

Plate 6 Adobe Pagemill HTML editor

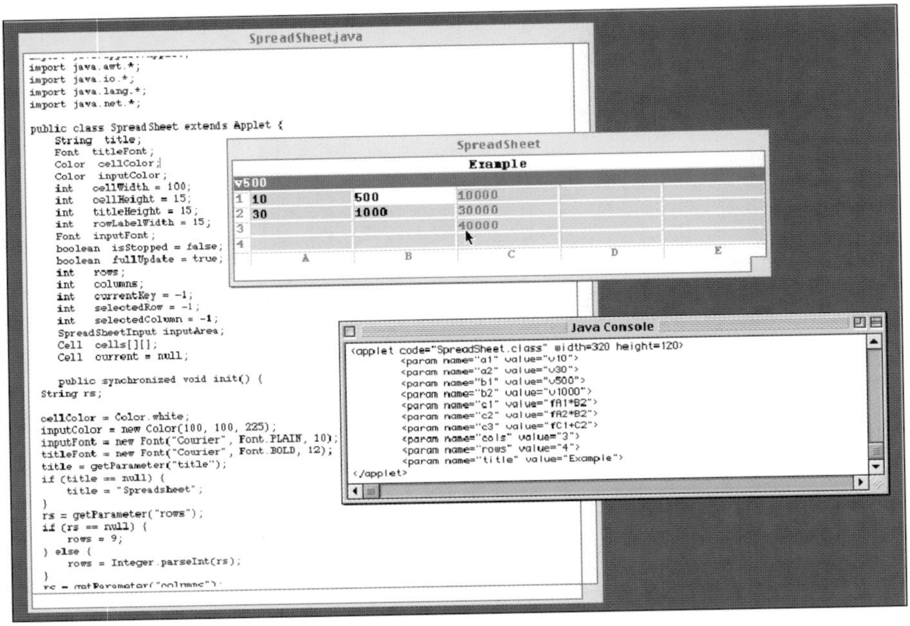

Plate 7 Example of a Java program

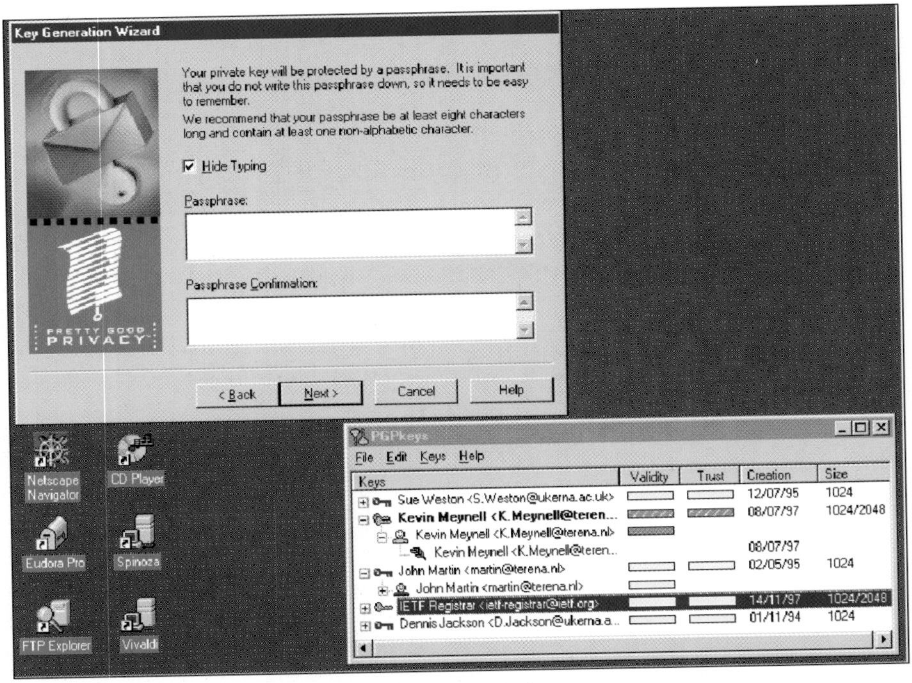

Plate 8 Pretty Good Privacy (PGP) client tools

`Countries` The list of members will be organized by the nationality taken from their email addresses.

`LOCal` LISTSERV lists can be peered (linked to other mailing lists of the same name but on different LISTSERV servers), and by default the `REView` command will include listings of all the mailing lists. The `LOCal` option restricts the scope of the `REView` command so that you receive a listing only from the server to which you send the `REView` command, and not its peers.

`Query list-name | *` When you join any mailing list, you will be assigned a default set of list options to control such things as how you will receive mail from the list, and the type of notification LISTSERV will give you when it distributes messages you have sent to a list (see the `SET` command for a complete description of these options and how to change them). The `Query` command can be used to review your personal list options. The `list-name` parameter is the name of a list to which you are subscribed. If you use an '`*`' (asterisk) character instead of a list name, you will receive information about your personal options for all lists to which you belong at the LISTSERV to which you send the command.

`SET list-name | * options` Use the `SET` command to change your personal options for a mailing list. The `list-name` parameter is the name of the mailing list for which you are changing your options. You may change your options for a specific list or for all the lists you belong to at a particular LISTSERV by using the '`*`' (asterisk) character in place of a list name. The important options are:

`Mail | DIGests | INDex | NOMail` These options alter the way in which you receive mail from a mailing list. The `Mail` option is the default, and means that you wish to have list mail distributed to you as mail. The `DIGests` and `INDex` options are available only if a list has had these features enabled by its owner(s). Digests hold all the mail messages sent to a list over a certain period of time. The `INDex` option will provide you with only the date, time, subject, number of lines and the sender's name and address for all mail messages sent to a list. The text of the mail message will not be included. You may then select and retrieve any mail that interests you from the list archive. The `NOMail` option means that you will no longer receive mail sent to the list.

`SHORThdr | FULLhdr | IETFhdr | DUALhdr` These options indicate the type of mail headers you want to include in the mail from a mailing list. `SHORThdr` means that only the essential mail headers will be included. This is the default. You may change this to `FULLhdr`, which means that all mail headers will be included. The `IETFhdr` option means that LISTSERV will not change the headers of a mail message it distributes, and is designed specifically for compatibility with SMTP (Simple Mail Transfer Protocol) exploders. Lastly, `DUALhdr` is very similar to the

SHORThdr option except that LISTSERV will also insert mail headers at the beginning of the mail body. This option is useful for users of some PC-based mail packages which do not display this information from the real mail headers.

CONCEAL | NOCONCEAL Indicates whether or not you want your name and mail address to appear in the display of list members which is given in response to a REView command. The default is NOCONCEAL. Note that a complete list of members is always given to list owners and LISTSERV administrators regardless of this option.

Commands for files

All files are stored in a hierarchical system of **filelists** which, as the name suggests, are special files each containing a **list of files**. Filelists contain details for each file such as the file's name, size and access code (**FAC**) which describes who is authorized to retrieve it.

The following LISTSERV commands enable general users to manipulate files stored at a server. File server commands to LISTSERV must be addressed to the server, not to any mailing lists. Where the PW= keyword appears in a command description, this need only be included in the command text if you have defined a personal password. The optional F= command keyword may be included as desired.

INDex <filelist> <F= format> Use the INDex command to get a listing of the files in a particular filelist. The filelist parameter can be used to specify a particular filelist; if no name is specified, an index of the root filelist (called LISTSERV FILELIST) will be sent to you.

GET filename filetype <filelist> <F= format> The GET command is used to retrieve a specific file or package from a filelist. You need authorization to do this. The filename and filetype parameters identify the file or package you wish to retrieve. The optional filelist parameter identifies the filelist within which the file or package resides; if this option is omitted, LISTSERV will determine the filelist through a search of its own internal filelist index.

Query File filename filetype <filelist> <(FLags> This command can be used to get update information on specified files and filetypes. You may specify a filelist name, but if you leave this out LISTSERV will locate the filelist through a search of its own internal filelist index. You may also specify the (FLags option to display additional technical data about the file (which can be useful when reporting problems to LISTSERV administrators).

PW options The PW command enables you to add, change or delete a personal password on any LISTSERV server. A personal password is designed to give you added command security, since it helps prevent impostors using your email address: for this reason the use of personal passwords is strongly encouraged. Passwords consist of one to eight alphanumeric characters. You may change or delete your password at any time. The options parameter must be one of the following:

`ADD new-password` Add a new personal password on the LISTSERV processing your command. Once you have registered a password on a LISTSERV server, you will be obliged to use the `PW=` command keyword in the commands where it appears as an option.

`CHange old-password new-password` Change your personal password on a LISTSERV server where you already have one.

`DELete old-password` Remove your personal password from a LISTSERV where you already have one. Once you have removed a password from a LISTSERV server, you will no longer be obliged to use the `PW=` command keyword in the commands where it appears as an option.

LISTSERV database functions

To find out what databases are accessible at a particular LISTSERV site, send the following command to that server:

```
DATABASE LIST
```

How you search a LISTSERV database using email depends on the version of the LISTSERV software which the server is running. For lists running on LISTSERV1.8c or later on Unix, VMS and Windows NT servers, an email message in this format can be sent to the server:

```
search <search terms> in <listname>
```

The response will be a message from the server listing the messages which relate to your search terms. You would then send an email with the command:

```
GETPOST <listname> <message numbers>
```

to obtain copies of the messages. It is also possible to search the archive via a World Wide Web interface if the list provides it.

Where the server is not one of the above, you can mail a `batch database job` to LISTSERV, containing your database query. You need to use precise syntax for the commands. Here is a template which may be used to search for messages containing a particular keyword in a specified mailing list:

```
// JOB Echo=No
Database Search DD=Rules
//Rules DD *
Search <keyword> in <listname> since <year>/<month>/<day>
Index
/*
```

Substitute as appropriate for <keyword>, <listname>, and <date> details and paste into your message.

You can get more detailed information on database functions and the database command syntax by requesting the file `LISTDB MEMO` from `LISTSERV@LISTSERV.NET` or from any other VM LISTSERV host. You can send either a `GET LISTDB MEMO` command or an `INFO DATABASE` command to retrieve the file. There is more information on the new 1.8c database functions in the *General User's Guide to LISTSERV 1.8c* available on L-Soft's WWW site at `http://www.lsoft.com/manuals/user/user.html`.

Commands for information

The LISTSERV server can provide a diverse range of information to the general user, including help files, release levels of the server and important configuration files, statistics and information pertaining to the EARN/Bitnet network. Requests for information must be addressed to the LISTSERV server and not to any mailing lists it may manage. When using commands that result in files being sent to the requestor (for example the `Info` command), the format of the file can be specified by the optional command keyword `F=` in the command text.

`Help` Use this command to get a brief description of the most commonly used LISTSERV commands and also the name and email address of the server's postmaster.

`Info <topic> <F= format>` Use this command to get a Help file from a LISTSERV server. You can specify a topic using the `topic` option; you can get a list of valid topics by sending the `Info` command with no parameters.

4.2 Usenet News

Usenet, sometimes called **Netnews**, is a huge collection of messages which are made available to users worldwide by means of the **UUCP** and **NNTP** protocols (**Unix to Unix Copy Program** and **Network News Transport Protocol**, respectively). Individual computing sites appoint somebody to oversee the huge quantity of incoming messages, and to decide how long messages can be kept before they must be removed to make room for new ones. Typically, messages are stored for less than a week. They are made available via a news server.

Access

Usenet newsgroups can be read at thousands of sites around the world. Users access local newsgroups with a **newsreader** program. Some WWW browsers come with an inbuilt newsreader or you may use a dedicated newsreader program. The newsreader accesses the local (or remote) News host using the Network News Transfer Protocol, enabling you to pull down as many newsgroups and their contents as you desire. If you don't have access locally to News, there is also a changeable list of publicly accessible Usenet hosts. If you don't know whether your site has Usenet access, check with your local computer support people.

Coverage

Every Usenet message belongs to a newsgroup; there are a few thousand of these, each containing messages on a particular subject. Users sending Usenet messages must address each message to a particular newsgroup. There are newsgroups on subjects ranging from education for the disabled to *Star Trek* and from environment science to politics in the former Soviet Union. The quality of the discussion in newsgroups may be excellent, but this is not guaranteed. Some newsgroups have a moderator who scans the messages for the group and decides which ones are appropriate for distribution.

Some of the newsgroups provide a useful source of information and help on technical topics. Users needing to find out about a subject often send questions to the appropriate newsgroup, and an expert somewhere in the world can often supply the answer. Lists of Frequently Asked Questions or FAQs are compiled and made available periodically in some newsgroups.

Using

Most, if not all, newsreaders provide the same basic functions:

- **Subscribing** to newsgroups: your news-reading software will make these groups immediately accessible, so that you can read their contents quickly and easily.
- **Unsubscribing** from newsgroups: removing groups from your easy access list.
- **Reading** newsgroup postings: your news reader presents new messages – postings – to you, and keeps track of which postings you have and have not read.
- **Threads of discussion**: replies to a posting are grouped together with the original posting, so that the reader can follow the messages within a newsgroup which are part of a particular discussion or a topic.
- **Posting** to newsgroups: you can participate in group discussions; your news reader knows where to send your posting.
- **Responding** to a posting: you can send a response to the newsgroup (often called **follow-up**) or to the author of a posting (often called **reply**).

Usenet newsgroups are themselves grouped into categories; eight of the major ones are called **alt**, **comp**, **misc**, **news**, **rec**, **sci**, **soc**, **talk**, standing for alternative, computing, miscellaneous, related to the news system itself, recreational, science, social and talk. The messages of many Bitnet LISTSERV mailing lists are also distributed in Usenet under the major category **bit**.

Other major categories based on particular subject areas (for example, bionet, biz, vmsnet) may be distributed worldwide as well, and there are categories based on geographical areas, on organizations (for example, ieee), or commercial interests (for example, clari). A fee is usually charged for access to commercial newsgroups.

Examples

When you enter the `tin` news reader, you get a listing of the newsgroups to which you are subscribed:

```
                         Group Selection (9)                h=help
    1 30637 bit.listserv.novell   local list
    2 1106 comp.mail.misc         General discussions about compu
    3 8031 comp.protocols.tcp-ip  TCP and IP network protocols.
    4 840 comp.sys.mac
    5 8789 news.answers           Repository for periodic USENET
 -> 6 29 news.lists               News-related statistics and lis
    7 15056 rec.woodworking       Hobbyists interested in woodwor
    8 7094 sci.psychology         Topics related to psychology.
    9 13093 soc.culture.celtic    Celtic, Irish, & Welsh culture
                          *** End of Groups ***
```

In `tin`, you select a newsgroup by using the arrow keys to move the -> sign alongside the newsgroup you are interested in, and press Return to select it. When you select a group, you get a listing of the articles:

```
                  comp.mail.misc (41T 64A 0K 0H)           h=help
    1 +   RIPEM Frequently Noted Vulnerabilities  Marc VanHeyningen
    2 +   RIPEM Frequently Asked Questions        Marc VanHeyningen
    3 +   Mail Archive Server software list       Jonathan I. Kamen
    4 + 1 UNIX Email Software Survey FAQ          Chris Lewis
    5 + 2 PC Eudora and Trumpet Winsock problem   Jim Graham
    6 +   X11 mail reader                         Dominique Marant
    7 +   MIME supporting e-mail                  Tim Goodwin
    8 + 1 IBM User name and Address Server        Wes Spears
    9 + 5 Newbie needs MHS/SMTP question answered Chris Pearce
   10 +   FAQ - pine                              Bruce Lilly
   11 +   FAQ: International E-mail accessibility Olivier M.J. Crep
-> 12 +   PC E-Mail and Dial-in                   Edward Vielmetti
   13 +   Prodigy Mail Manager 01/07            an33127@anon.pene
   14 +   Prodigy Mail Manager 02/07            an33127@anon.pene
   15 +   Prodigy Mail Manager 03/07            an33127@anon.pene
```

`tin` is a **threaded** news reader, which means that replies to a posting are grouped together with the original posting, so that the reader can follow a thread of discussion. The list above shows the threads, the number of replies in each thread, the subject and the author. The plus sign (+) indicates that not all postings in the thread have been read. Other news readers show other details.

Use the arrow keys to move the -> sign alongside the thread you are interested in, and then press Return to select it. The messages in that thread will appear on your screen:

```
Wed, 01 Sep 1993 07:05:49     comp.mail.misc     Thread 13 of 41
Lines 27             Re: PC E-Mail and Dial-in         No responses
emv@garnet.msen.com  Edward Vielmetti at Msen, Inc. -- Ann Arbor

Sherry H. Lake (slake@mason1.gmu.edu) wrote:

:    I am looking for an email package that will allow a user to
: dial-in to his mail machine download any messages to his local
: PC, delete the messages from the server and then automatically
: sign him off. The user can then use his client software (local)
: to read, compose and reply. He then would have to dial-in again
: to so his outgoing mail will be uploaded to the server.
Various POP clients for PCs or Windows Sockets will do roughly
this. You should look at:
-   NUPOP (MS-DOS)
-   Eudora for Windows (Windows)
-   WinQVT/Net (Windows)
-   various commercial POP clients listed in the 'alt.winsock'
    directory of commercial Windows systems

You'll want to look particularly for dial up IP software (SLIP or
PPP) that makes the process of connecting minimally onerous, e.g.
by scripting the session so that the users don't have to type
anything, perhaps by automatically dialing for you when you go to
read or otherwise open a network connection, and offering a
reasonable way to disconnect.

Edward Vielmetti, vice president for research, Msen Inc.
emv@Msen.com Msen Inc., 628 Brooks, Ann Arbor MI 48103
+1 313 998 4562 (fax: 998 4563)
```

Finding more information

News programs communicate with each other according to standard protocols, some of which are described by RFCs (Internet Request For Comments).

Copies of RFCs are often posted to the network and obtainable from archive sites. Current news-related RFCs include the following:

- **RFC 977** specifies NNTP, the Network News Transfer Protocol,
- **RFC 1036** specifies the format of Usenet articles.

Some newsgroups carry articles and discussions on the use of Usenet, notably: **news.announce.newusers**, **news.answers** and **news.newusers.questions.**

Many of the articles which appear periodically in these newsgroups or in others are also available from `rtfm.mit.edu` by anonymous ftp or by mail to `mail-server@rtfm.mit.edu`.

4.3 Web conferencing

Web conferencing is a means for interest groups to exchange information and opinions via the Web. Using the WWW they can contribute messages, as well as read previous messages in a conference. Like other Internet forums, Web conferencing can be a working tool for specialist work teams, a support mechanism for sufferers, a casual forum for hobbyists, and many other things besides. Its particular strength is that it uses the Web, which is something most Internet users will already be familiar with, and which provides a cross-platform, low-cost means of hosting an ongoing discussion, potentially available to readers and contributors anywhere on the Internet or Intranet.

Like so many other Internet systems, Web conferences operate on the client–server model. There is a server which takes care of the administration of the conference and maintains the files of messages and subscriptions. And there is a client, which is the program which the user uses to access the Web conference. This will usually be a regular Web browser such as Netscape Navigator or Internet Explorer, though some Web conferencing systems require their own client software, or use plug-ins to a regular Web browser. Whichever it is, the interface to a Web conference is generally very simple and intuitive.

Web conferencing in practice

A Web conference may be entered via a login process. This enables the conference server to keep a record of where users have been and a note of their preferences. Once through the initial process, the user will normally see on the Web page a list of the topics in a conference, possibly with an indication of the number of responses within each topic. From there, the reader can select a topic and browse through the messages.

Some systems allow for subscriptions to particular topics so that a user will see a personally customized view of the conference when he or she logs in. Users can then go straight into the discussions which interest them most. The system may also indicate for each topic the number of messages added since the user's last visit.

The interface may provide additional features such as grouping messages by hierarchies of subtopics (threads), the possibility of sorting messages by subject/date/author and a search facility. Web conferences can be made private through password access. The submission of new messages is normally handled through a Web form and passed to the server by a CGI script. Java is another means for handling these interactive functions though this may limit access from browsers which are not Java-enabled.

Software

There is a great deal of software for Web conferencing systems available, a considerable amount of which is free. A few examples are included in the descriptive list in Section 4.5.2. For an extensive list which points to examples of use, see Woolley, D.: *Conferencing on the World Wide Web: A guide to software that powers discussion forums on the Web* at `http://freenet.msp.mn.us/people/drwool/`.

To read more about Web conferencing, see the Bibliography.

4.4 Real-time multimedia communication

Real-time multimedia communication implies interactive communication using media other than print, obvious examples being audioconferencing and videoconferencing which are the main focus here. Access to audioconferencing and videoconferencing via the Internet is improving at a rapid rate at present. Though network capacity and speed is always an issue with bandwidth-hungry applications like this, more people have access to the high-speed connections which are a prerequisite for quality multimedia communication, and also there are more and better tools to choose from all the time. Combining audio and video communication with facilities such as document and application sharing or whiteboards, provides a powerful mechanism for group collaboration, distance learning and other areas of application.

4.4.1 Videoconferencing

Videoconferencing can be used in a variety of ways:

- one-to-one, that is, one person with another;
- one-to-many, that is, broadcast to many sites, for instance a lecture;

- many-to-many, that is, more than two parties take part. Some applications switch the active video transmission from one to the other as required.

4.4.2 Internet phone

Most Internet phone tools are point-to-point, though at least one allows conferences of multiple calls. Many of the vendors of Internet phone software maintain a server which keeps details such as email address and IP number for users of the service. They also group users according to their stated interests facilitating contact between users with common interests. Calls are made through the server or direct if the IP address is known.

4.4.3 From studio to desktop PC

One of the reasons that good quality multimedia communication over the networks has been an elusive goal is the sheer size of video and audio files and the limited capacity of network pipes. Because video and audio are so time-dependent, on a slow link bits of data which don't arrive in time get dropped. The result is jerky video or strange-sounding speech. Compressing the data alleviates the problem, but a lot of computing power is required to process the compression and decompression of the files. The best quality videoconferencing has to date been accomplished with expensive custom-designed suites of hardware which come with their own compression/decompression (codec) hardware. But as technology moves on, PCs on the desktop are catching up in processing power with the supercomputers of yesterday. Methods of data compression are smarter too. And networks are upgrading all the time. Much can be accomplished with the use of specialist application software with inbuilt compression. Also, videoconferencing and audioconferencing applications increasingly conform to international standards, which means that more people can talk to each other, no matter which computer or which software they are using. The end result is that desktop videoconferencing and Internet phoning are increasingly viable, and it seems likely that video- and audio-conferencing will be seen as standard functions of the desktop PC in the future.

For a clear explanation of the technical issues related to desktop videoconferencing, consult the paper by Rhett D. Hudson at `http://www.visc.vt.edu/succeed/videoconf.html`.

4.4.4 Standards

One of the lynchpins of effective videoconferencing and audioconferencing between people using different computers and different software is the use of common standards. The main standard for Internet videoconferencing is H.323, and many new products are advertising that they are H.323

compliant. This is an important feature to watch for when getting set up for videoconferencing. H.324 is the equivalent standard for ISDN.

4.4.5 Networks

Videoconferencing can be used over the following different types of networks:

- Local Area Networks (LANs) such as university networks;
- Wide Area Networks (WANs) such as national networks and the wider Internet;
- the MBone (Multicast Backbone), a virtual network layered on top of parts of the Internet, designed for efficient transmission of real-time multimedia using multicast.

In the research and academic world, users will most likely access a videoconference from their networked computer on a LAN connected to the Internet. Many of the tools now appearing are designed for, or adapted to, Internet protocols. ISDN (Integrated Services Digital Network), for which there are many commercial videoconferencing products available, may also be used. There are also products which claim to be usable with a modem connection, 28.8K being the minimum tolerable speed.

4.4.6 MBone

The MBone (see Plate 4) has been described as 'an experimental worldwide digital radio and television service for the Internet' (Tanenbaum, 1996). It is a response to the problem of delivering real-time multimedia applications such as videoconferencing in an Internet environment where data is chopped and spliced and left to make its way through variable and narrow routes to its destination, perhaps arriving in time to become one whole again, perhaps not.

The MBone uses a protocol designed to ensure that packets do arrive in time so that the video or audio streams in smoothly. It also addresses the problem of limited bandwidth. The 'M' in MBone stands for **multicast**, which is a technique for efficiently broadcasting real-time data over the network without saturating the bandwidth. Only one copy of a multicast message will pass over any link in the network but it will still be available to any (MBone-enabled) local area network which opts to receive it, and from there distributed to users wishing to take part. Because adding users needn't impose extra load on the network, this technology can support many recipients. Given an adequate supply of bandwidth, it is particularly well suited for real-time multimedia communication. But given that bandwidth on the Internet cannot be guaranteed, quality remains an issue.

The MBone originated in an experiment to multicast audio and video from the Internet Engineering Task Force (IETF) meetings and continued as a medium for research and testing of multicast protocols and services. The potential of multicast technology is beginning to be realized by a wider community and the large and growing body of users now includes commercial sites as well as research and education sites.

Access

In order to use the MBone, you need to be on a network which has multicast routing enabled. The MBone is really a virtual network running over parts of the Internet, connecting up multicast-enabled local networks and workstations, and using its own software, routers and class of IP addresses.

MBone sessions may use video, audio, shared whiteboard, text editor, and so on and IP multicast application software for these will need to be installed. Applications for a number of platforms are available. While Unix workstations have been the norm in the past, most people will begin to use these applications on PCs running Windows. Some of the commonly used ones include:

- **sdr** – session announcements,
- **vat** – audioconferencing,
- **vic** – videoconferencing,
- **wb** – shared whiteboard,
- **nt** – text editor.

See the descriptive list of MBone tools in Section 4.4.8 for more information.

Coverage

The MBone can be used for many different types of events and data. Commonly it is used to broadcast technical meetings such as those of the IETF. Notable variations from this pattern include the NASA space shuttle launches, a Rolling Stones concert, courses of lectures, and other live meetings and performances. Multicast technology is well suited to applications in the commercial area too, for example the transmission of stored data streams such as updates of kiosks or video-server-to-video-server updates, as well as transfer of large databases such as stock/commodities quotes and trading information.

Using

Graphical interface

Sdr provides an easy interface for accessing the MBone and all the actions necessary to join a session can be done from here. Its focal point is a menu of sessions currently on offer. A mouse click on one of these enables you to join it and automatically start up the relevant tools for videoconferencing, audio, whiteboard or whatever is being used in the session.

When setting up a session yourself, you can check *sdr*'s calendar to see which other sessions are scheduled so as to avoid a clash. You need to provide some basic details on your planned session, decide whether it is to be confined to your site or region or whether it should be worldwide. You can also nominate the format to be used for audio, video, and so on. Once you've made your selections, the planned session will be listed in *sdr*'s menu of sessions and available for others to join.

Command line interface

If you need to use a plain Unix command line interface to the tools, the standard formula is:

```
name_of_tool -t ttl [other flags]
multicast_address/port_number
```

`ttl` is the time to live, which effectively specifies the range of the session, for example

- set `ttl` to 16 to keep the session within your own site;
- set `ttl` to 47 to keep the session within the UK;
- set `ttl` to 63 for a European conference;
- set `ttl` to 127 for worldwide access.

Another useful flag is `-N`, which allows you to enter your name. An example of the command to start `nt` is:

```
nt -t 16 -N "Your name" 224.2.501.678/45678 &
```

Examples

A videoconference of a scientific meeting is announced on the MBone using the tool *sdr*. MBone users everywhere can use *sdr* on their MBone-enabled workstation to see the announcement of this videoconference. The announcement will give details of the timing of the conference and the media being used, for example audio, video and shared whiteboard. At the announced time, the broadcast takes place. Interested users will then access *sdr* again and launch the application software needed for the conference, in this case *vat vic* and *wb*. If they have the appropriate video and audio hardware installed, they will be able to see and hear the speakers in the conference, and see their slides via the shared whiteboard. They will also be able to see a list of other participants in the conference. If the session is opened up for questions, they may be able to ask a question using the audio tool and take part in the subsequent discussion – all in real-time.

Finding more information

The MBone Information Web at http://www.mbone.com/

IP Multicast Initiative: How IP Multicast Works (White Paper) at http://www.ipmulticast.com/community/whitepapers/howipmcworks.htm

Introduction to Videoconferencing and the Mbone at http://www-itg.lbl.gov/~clarsen/vconf/vconf-faq.html

Mike Macedonia and Don Brutzman: *MBONE, the Multicast BackbONE* at http://www-mice.cs.ucl.ac.uk/mice/mbone_review.html

MICE National Support Centre User documentation at http://www-mice.cs.ucl.ac.uk/mice-nsc/tools/. (Includes links to Installation and User Guides for MBone tools.)

Table of multicast compatible products at http://www.ipmulticast.com/ipmi_dir/quick_view.html

4.4.7 Getting ready for videoconferencing

Hardware

To use videoconferencing on your networked computer, you will need:

- a video card
- a camera
- a full duplex audio card
- a microphone
- speakers.

Some systems also require a plug-in (codec) board to handle the compression/decompression. Others use the computer's normal processor plus special purpose software. The hardware solution (the plug-in board) is likely to give better quality, but will also be more expensive.

High-end workstations such as those from Sun, Silicon Graphics, DEC and HP are well suited to videoconferencing. Many of them have inbuilt facilities for sound, video and multicast access, as well as operating systems and processor power which meet the demanding requirements of quality video. To use a PC for videoconferencing, a 90 MHz Pentium running Windows 95 or NT is about the minimum configuration. A good VGA adaptor is necessary for the video display.

Software

There are many videoconferencing applications available both for the high-end workstations and for ordinary desktop computers.

One of the most accessible tools providing low-cost desktop videoconferencing is CUSeeMe, though sound and picture quality here may not be first class. Multicasting provides an alternative technology via the MBone which users can access from MBone-linked multicast-capable machines. A number of MBone tools are listed in Section 4.4.8.

4.4.8 Client software for real-time multimedia communication

MBone tools

The following MBtools require a system which supports IP Multicast connected to an IP Multicast network.

sdr

Sdr is a tool for announcing and scheduling multimedia conferences on the Mbone. Users can use *sdr* to see what conferences are available and to join them. They can also use it to announce conferences and to specify timing, media and other details. Sessions can be either public or private and may optionally link to further information on the Web.

Features

- Making and receiving session announcements,
- use of encryption for secure session announcements,
- built-in World Wide Web browser.

Access For information on setting up *sdr*, see MICE: Installing sdr at `http://www-mice.cs.ucl.ac.uk/mice-nsc/tools/install-sdr.html`. For more information see The sdr Session Directory at `http://ugwww.ucs.ed.ac.uk/mice/archive/sdr.html`.

vat

Vat is a real-time, multiparty, multimedia application for audioconferencing over the Internet. While *vat* is used as an independent audioconferencing tool, it is frequently used as the audio part of a full videoconference.

Features

- Audio conferencing: one-to-one, one-to-many, many-to-many,
- control over local audio,
- details of participants,
- logging.

Access Sound-capable workstation and microphone required. Also the *vat* software must be installed. Source code and binaries in LBL ftp archive at `ftp://ftp.ee.lbl.gov/conferencing/vat/alpha-test/`. See also MICE User

Guide to vat at http://www-mice.cs.ucl.ac.uk/mice-nsc/tools/user-vat.html and vat – LBNL Audio Conferencing Tool at http://www-nrg.ee.lbl.gov/vat/vat.html.

vic

Vic is a videoconferencing tool which provides the video portion of a multimedia conference. Although *vic* can be run for one-to-one conferences, it is primarily intended as a multiparty conferencing application. It can be used in different computing environments and can accommodate both lower and higher bandwidth conditions.

Features

- 'Intra-H.261' video encoder,
- voice activated viewing (the viewing window follows the speaker),
- multiple dithering algorithms,
- interactive 'title generation',
- routing of decoded video to external video ports.

Access FTP Archive at ftp://ftp.ee.lbl.gov/conferencing/vic/; Version for Win 32 at http://www.cs.ucl.ac.uk/staff/I.Kouvelas/vic/. Video camera and video capture card in order to send video. For more information see Vic – videoconferencing tool at http://ugwww.ucs.ed.ac.uk/mice/archive/vic.html.

rat

Rat (Robust Audio Tool) is an audio tool developed for use in multimedia conferencing. It was designed to be robust to packet loss and adaptive to both host and network conditions.

Features

- *Rat* contains features which attempt to compensate for lost and misordered packets.

Access See the Tutorial for RAT at http://www-mice.cs.ucl.ac.uk/mice-nsc/tools/rat-tut/RAThomepage.html and The RAT Home Page at http://www-mice.cs.ucl.ac.uk/mice/rat/.

wb

Wb is the shared whiteboard tool. For meetings it provides a normal shared whiteboard on which participants may write, draw and type with all contributions visible to all participants. In a seminar it can be an OHP by using its capacity to import PostScript pages.

Features

- Drawing tools,
- keyboard input of text,

- formatting of text,
- information on other participants,
- import of PostScript pages,
- saving and printing current page,
- multiple pages.

Access MICE National Support Centre: User Guide to wb at `http://www-mice.cs.ucl.ac.uk/mice-nsc/tools/user-wb.html`.

nt

Nt (NetText editor) is a shared text editor designed to enable a number of people to edit a document simultaneously (though not the same line). It is most appropriate when used as part of a multimedia conference in which it is a support tool.

Features

- Simultaneous editing of a block of text.

Access For further information see About NetText at `http://ugwww.ucs.ed.ac.uk/mice/archive/nt.html`.

IP/TV MBONE Viewer

IP/TV MBONE Viewer is a low-priced version of Precept's IP/TV for users in the academic and research communitites wishing to access the MBone from a PC running Windows. The Viewer delivers full-motion video to the desktop PC.

Features

- Full-motion video display,
- synchronized audio,
- lists scheduled MBone programs,
- IETF standards compliant.

Access MBone Program Guide available on Precept Web site. Pentium processor running Windows 95 or NT (Windows 3.11 requires Win32S software), TCP/IP stack with support for IP Multicasting and IGMP protocol. Further details from Precept Web Site at `http://www.precept.com/`.

Other tools

CUSeeMe

CUSeeMe is a desktop videoconferencing program for real-time person-to-person or group conferencing on the Internet and Intranets. The latest version of White Pine's CUSeeMe provides for multiparty conferences of up to 12 people. Multiparty conferences are hosted on a conference server (a **reflector**) which transmits video and sound to and from all participants.

Quality may not be first class but it is groundbreaking in making this technology accessible to a large number of users at relatively low cost. It can even be used with a 28.8K or higher modem connection.

Features

- Colour videoconferencing,
- audioconferencing,
- Chat,
- whiteboard,
- address book,
- multicast support,
- H.323 compliant.

Access Commercial version from WhitePine Software at `http://www.cuseeme.com/`. Versions for Windows 3.*/95/NT, Macintosh and Power Macintosh also from White Pine Software. Free version of CUSeeMe from the original developers at Cornell University's CUSeeMe Page at `http://cu-seeme.cornell.edu/`.

VDOPhone Internet

VDOPhone Internet is full-colour, motion video and audio software that uses the Internet and a personal computer equipped with Windows 95 and the right system requirements to link you directly to another VDOPhone (or compatible) user. VDOPhone Internet dynamically adjusts for the frequent and rapid changes in the bandwidth of a typical Internet connection. It is designed to give the audio stream priority so that even in low bandwidth connections, the sound will come through clearly.

Features

- Full-colour, motion video,
- two-way video and audio communication,
- can be used in conjunction with Microsoft's NetMeeting,
- online directory of users.

Access Pentium processor with Windows 95, and standard videoconferencing requirements. Further information from VDOPhone Web page at `http://www.vdo.net/vdostore/overview.html`.

Apple VideoPhone Kit

Apple VideoPhone Kit is an audioconferencing and collaboration package, comprising colour camera, videoconferencing and collaboration software, System Software 7.5.5, Farallon's Timbuktu Pro for document sharing, and an integrated AppleGuide. Using Apple VideoPhone Kit, you can audioconference with other users of Apple VideoPhone products, as well as cross-platform with Windows, Unix, and Macintosh users who are using Netscape's CoolTalk audioconferencing products.

Features

- Limited video with a 28.8 modem,
- full capabilities including videoconference with a faster network connection,
- supports international standards,
- video capture and playback software,
- built-in access to online directory service,
- shared whiteboard,
- file transfer.

Access Available from Apple resellers. More details from the Apple VideoPhone Products Web page at `http://qtc.quicktime.apple.com/qtc/qtc.AVP.html`.

ProShare

Client software for full featured video conferencing over ISDN and LAN/WAN.

Features

- Videoconferencing,
- whiteboard,
- photo exchange,
- file transfer.

Access Windows 95; Windows NT. Intel Business Video Conferencing page at `http://www.intel.com/proshare/conferencing/index.htm`.

References

Multimedia Conferencing Applications Archive at `http://ugwww.ucs.ed.ac.uk/mice/archive/`

4.5 Collaboration tools

Collaboration via the Internet is currently the focus of much attention and development. New and improved tools are enabling workgroups to use the networks effectively for discussion and decision-making, for holding meetings, for working on documents, for one-to-one or group conversations, for scheduling workflow and a range of other tasks. There is much ongoing development including a number of research projects such as Web4Groups at `http://www.web4groups.at/w4g/project/index.html` and BSCW (Basic Support for Cooperative Work), and CoBrow (Collaborative Browsing of Information Resources) at `http://www.tik.ee.ethz.ch/~cobrow/overview/welcome.html`.

Many of the new collaboration tools are provided on a server and accessed with a WWW browser. Some are also available using browser plug-ins, or using special-purpose client software. A significant current trend is the emergence of collaboration packages which provide a whole suite of facilities for collaboration purposes. Some of these have been adapted for the Internet from standard groupware applications such as Lotus Notes. Others are new products designed specifically for Internet and Intranet use, for example AltaVista Forum (see Section 4.5.2). As well as the composite collaboration packages, there is a vast amount of single-purpose application software available, such as Web conferencing systems, Chat clients, videoconferencing tools, phone tools, and so on. It is notable that the two major Web browsers from Netscape and Microsoft now come with a bundle of programs for collaboration purposes.

Broadly the most common functions available in collaboration tools are:

- group exchange of text messages,
- multimedia exchanges (audio and video),
- document/application sharing,
- whiteboard.

Additional functions may include:

- collaborative browsing of WWW documents,
- annotation of WWW documents,
- voting and rating,
- tracking workflow,
- calendar sharing.

4.5.1 Common collaborative functions

Exchange of text messages

The common feature is that messages are typed and sent. Within that context, there are a few broad variations that may be understood effectively through analogy as described below.

Exchanges that resemble conversations

A message is sent and displayed immediately it is transmitted, the receiver responds, this is followed by a counter-response, and so on, and so on. Each message is immediately available to all participants and they experience the dialogue as it happens, that is, in real-time.

Examples Chat is a tool for interactive exchange of plain-text messages. The foremost example is the public Chat system Internet Relay Chat (IRC) which has a large following. But public discussions on IRC are not the only route for using Chat services. It is possible to set up private discussions and many organizations run their own Chat services. A Chat facility is available in many different packages, for example Netscape's Conference and Microsoft's NetMeeting, as well as specialist Chat clients such as mIRC or Mirabilis ICQ. See Section 4.5.2.

Exchanges that are like posting a message on a notice board
Messages on notice boards can be posted at any time and will stay in place until people come to read them. This type of exchange operates in a similar way. A plain-text message is sent to a group. It can be responded to with further messages posted in the same place. The timing doesn't matter as the dialogue doesn't depend on immediate responses. Past messages can be systematically archived and browsed and may also be searchable.

Examples Web conferencing and Usenet News are examples of this type of functionality.

Real-time multimedia communication

This covers audio exchanges such as phone conversations, and audio/video exchanges such as audioconferencing and videoconferencing. Exchanges may be one-to-one or involve a group of participants. Multimedia exchanges are big bandwidth users and may not be practicable with a regular modem connection.

Examples See Section 4.4.8 for a descriptive list of tools.

Document/application sharing

Co-workers can view and edit documents stored in a common area (a **shared workspace**). Documents are updated as edits occur. Usually this will require each participant to have the application with which the document was produced, such as a word processor or spreadsheet application. Documents should only be able to be changed by those with appropriate access privileges.

Examples BSCW offers shared workspaces for exchanging documents of any kind. Microsoft's NetMeeting offers document and application sharing. See Section 4.5.2.

Whiteboard

A whiteboard facility allows a group of collaborators to collectively create a document such as a list of priority items or a plan of action. The document is edited using mouse or keyboard. Locally the whiteboard program looks like a simple drawing package, but in a live session, changes made to it by any participant appear on every participant's machine.

Examples Whiteboard facilities are available as part of Microsoft's NetMeeting and Netscape's Conference. For more details see Section 4.5.2.

4.5.2 Client software for collaboration

Multifunction collaboration packages

AltaVista Forum
AltaVista Forum is an application for group collaboration. It includes a suite of programs for communication and document sharing with flexible provision for controlled access.

Features

- Web conferencing,
- Chat,
- sharing documents,
- group calendar,
- searching Internet news sources and sharing the results.

Access Forum runs on a server and is accessed with a Web browser. Details of the cost of the server software plus a 60-day trial copy are available free from AltaVista's Forum site at `http://altavista.software.digital.com/forum/index.htm`.

Microsoft NetMeeting
NetMeeting consists of a suite of client programs which enable talking (video and audio) and exchanging messages in real-time over the net, working on documents and a whiteboard, and exchanging files. Conferences are organized by connecting initially to a directory server.

Features

- Audio- and videoconferencing (two people),
- document/application sharing (three people),
- whiteboard,
- Chat,
- file transfer,
- conference switch from one person to another,
- H.323 compliant.

Access Available free from Microsoft. Platforms: Windows 95 or NT. Video requires a video-capture card and camera. Audio requires a sound card, microphone and speakers. Versions for many languages. See also Microsoft: Complete Communication & Collaboration at `http://www.microsoft.com/ie/ie40/collab/netmtg.htm`.

Netscape Conference
Netscape Conference (see Plate 5) is a composite communications package integrated into Netscape Communicator. Conference includes real-time tools for talking, exchanging messages and working on a shared whiteboard.

Features

- Audioconferencing,
- whiteboard,
- Chat,
- collaborative browsing,
- sending voicemail,
- file transfer,
- personalized address book,
- H.323 compliant.

Access Netscape Software download page at `http://home.netscape.com/download/index.html` (Communicator Complete Install). Versions for Windows 3.1, Windows 95 and Windows NT and Macintosh PowerPC and 68K. Free for educational and non-profit organization members, and for others for a 90-day evaluation period. For cost details see the Netscape download pages. See also Netscape Conference Home Page at `http://home.netscape.com/comprod/products/communicator/conference.html`.

Lotus Domino
Groupware and email server for the Web provide a forum for individuals and groups to collaborate, share information and coordinate business activities. Used for building collaborative applications, enterprise-scalable messaging, calendaring and scheduling, and a secure interactive Web site.

Features

- Web site tools,
- object store,
- search engine,
- dynamic documents,
- managing and securing applications made easy,
- tight security provision,
- replication of information,
- messaging with calendaring and scheduling,
- integration with relational databases through ODBC,
- distribution and tracking of documents,
- agent software.

Access Access to the Domino server is possible with a variety of clients and devices, including Web browsers, Notes clients, and POP3 and other mail clients. Server runs on Windows NT (Intel and Alpha), Sun Solaris SPARC and Intel Edition, AIX, HP-UX, OS/2.

For trial purposes, Domino can be downloaded free of charge from the Lotus Notes site at `http://www.notes.net/`. Purchase through traditional reseller channels or through Lotus's business partner network.

Communique!
Communique! is a suite of programs for cross-platform collaboration via the network. Its functionality can scale according to need, ranging from application sharing and whiteboarding to a full-function collaborative and videoconferencing solution. Functionality can be added to using the InSoft OpenDVE application development toolkit.

Features

- Real-time interactive sessions for multiple users,
- high quality audio/video synchronization,
- whiteboard,
- file transfer,
- Chat,
- intuitive user interface.

Access Available for a range of platforms from Sun SPARCStation through to PC Pentium. Further details from the InSoft site at `http://www.insoft.com`.

Document/application sharing

BSCW
BSCW (Basic Support for Cooperative Work) enables collaboration over the Web. BSCW is a 'shared workspace' system which supports document upload, event notification, group management and much more.

Features

- Shared workspaces for exchanging documents,
- download and upload via Web browser,
- workspace keeps you aware of changes,
- server available in a number of languages.

Access To access a workspace you only need a standard Web browser. To create your own workspaces you can use the public server at GMD at `http://bscw.gmd.de/`. Alternatively, you can install your own server at your site. The server software (for Unix or Windows NT) is free and can be downloaded from the BSCW Download page at `http://bscw.gmd.de/DownloadServer.html`.

Web conferencing

Allaire Forums
Web conferencing application which works with Cold Fusion, Allaire's Web application development software. Forums offers interactive discussion via the Web. Messages are posted to the conference via Web forms, and archives of discussion are viewed with a Web browser.

Features

- Message exchange,
- archiving of messages and threads,
- full-text searching of archive,
- subscription to threads to receive new messages via email,
- file exchange,
- configurable interface,
- sophisticated security framework.

Access Conference participants need only use a Web browser. Server can be purchased from Allaire. Runs on Windows NT or Windows 95 Web server. Further details of price, availability and system requirements from `http://www.allaire.com/`.

Caucus

Web conferencing software with user access to conferences via a Web browser.

Features

- Threads within a conference,
- search facility,
- password access to conference,
- membership lists,
- messages posted from Web page via forms.

Access Conferences are accessed with a plain Web browser. Server software available for a range of Unix systems from the Screen Portch site at `http://screenporch.com/`. 30-day trial version available for free, purchase thereafter.

Chat

Mirabilis ICQ

ICQ is a chat client for chatting with other ICQ users. This exclusivity provides additional functionality and a tool well suited for private forums. You can set up your own list of correspondents from whom you will accept chat requests. When they are registered with the service, the program alerts you when they are online. When set up ICQ stays resident in the background until called upon. Chat sessions and other services are managed by the Mirabilis server.

Features

- Chat with one or more users,
- private sessions,
- will launch third-party applications such as Internet phone applications,

- file transfer and file server facility,
- automatic exchange of URLs,
- paging service,
- saves messages received while user is offline.

Access The ICQ software must be downloaded from the Mirabilis site at `http://www.mirabilis.com` and installed. Versions available for Windows and Apple Mac.

mIRC

Shareware IRC chat program for Windows which offers a highly configurable, user-friendly interface to IRC together with additional options and tools such as support of Web tours, making files available via ftp, a finger facility, support for sorting, searching and filtering of channels, firewall support and other features.

Features

- Chat,
- file transfer,
- aliases,
- WWW and sound support,
- firewall support.

Access Available from many sites around the world including Demon in the UK at `ftp://ftp.demon.co.uk/pub/ibmpc/win3/winsock/apps/mirc/` and the Finnish ftp archive at `ftp://ftp.funet.fi/pub/msdos/networks/irc/windows/`. Free for a 30-day evaluation period, then registration fee is required. Versions for Windows 95, Windows 3.x (with the win32s 32-bit extensions).

References

Woolley, D.: *Conferencing on the World Wide Web: A guide to software that powers discussion forums on the Web* at `http://freenet.msp.mn.us/people/drwool/`.

4.5.3 IRC (Internet Relay Chat)

IRC (Internet Relay Chat) is a real-time conversational system which allows two or more users to communicate interactively via typed messages. As a message is typed, it is immediately transmitted and displayed for each person taking part in the conversation. Though the medium is plain text, IRC offers live dialogue over the net which is within the reach of most network users.

Access

Like many other Internet tools, IRC is a client–server system. IRC is hosted on a server, to which users connect using a Chat client. There are many dedicated clients available such as mIRC and PIRCH. For a list of dedicated clients by platform, see `http://www.wildstar.net/irc/clients/`.

Chat client software may come as part of a Web browser package, for example the Conference component of Netscape Communicator or Microsoft NetMeeting. Some Chat services are accessed using Java. For these, you will need a Java-capable Web browser such as Netscape Navigator 2.0 or later or Internet Explorer 3.0 or later.

The first thing to do when you start using IRC is to select the IRC server to which you will connect. A list of servers may be included with your client software. There is also the *Index of Server Lists* at `http://www.irchelp.org/irchelp/networks/servers/index.htm`.

Coverage

IRC servers link together to form networks that cover much of the world. There are many IRC networks including regional and private networks. The three most notable public ones are called EFnet, UnderNet and DALnet. The EfNet is the original and biggest IRC network.

Topics of discussion on IRC are varied. Technical and political discussions are popular, especially concerning current world events. There are many purely recreational discussions going on all the time (see a list of channels on Yahoo). IRC may be a way to expand your horizons, as people from many countries and cultures are on the system, 24 hours a day. Most conversations are in English, but there are always channels in German, Finnish, Japanese, and occasionally other languages.

Using

Fundamental to the operation of IRC is the **channel**: each channel is one conversation. The number of channels is essentially unlimited. Channels have several characteristics in addition to their name. They can be private, invite-only, limited membership, moderated, and so on. If you don't find a channel which suits you, you can create your own.

When you start using IRC, you first select a server to connect to, then nominate one or more nicknames which you will use. You then need to join a channel to start chatting. Your presence will be made known to the others on the channel and everything you type will be seen by them. They can then respond to your messages.

Additional flexibility is provided via commands, enabling you, for instance, to run a parallel conversation with a particular user. The commands are available either from your client's menu, or by typing, depending on the interface you are using. All typed IRC commands begin with a slash, for example /HELP for Help, /LIST for a list of available channels.

Examples

Our first example is *Talk.com* on the HotWired site http://talk.com/. *Talk.com* is a Java-based Internet Chat system for HotWired members (membership is free). (If your browser does not support Java, you can enter *Talk.com* by telnetting directly to talk.com.) You will need to register to use *Talk.com* unless you are already a HotWired member. After that, give yourself a nickname which will be used for your Chat session. Then select a 'Chat room', that is, a topic-related conversation. When you enter the 'room', *Talk.com* displays the last ten sentences spoken in that room, whether the conversation happened a minute ago or an hour ago. The name of the room you are currently in always appears on the Chat window's title bar. Next to the Chat area is a list of all the rooms currently available. Highlighting and clicking on a room name will tell you how many people are chatting in that room and what their nicknames are. To change rooms, highlight the room you wish to visit and click Go to Room.

You can request a private Chat with any member by highlighting that person's name and clicking Private Chat. If the person you requested a Chat with accepts, a new Chat area will open up with just the two of you in it. Either of you can disconnect from this private Chat area at any time.

Another example is *Yahoo! Chat* at http://chat.yahoo.com/. This service provides continuous Chat channels which you can join, using only your Web browser if you wish. You will be asked to register before starting, and will be given the choice of using a plug-in (iChat), Java, or HTML. If you want to use the plug-in, you will first need to download and install it, which is very simple and straightforward. Once you are set up, you can join in a discussion. Channels are grouped under broad categories such as Science, Computers, Sport, and so on. You can see a list of channels within each category, and how many people are currently in them. Select any one to join it and you will immediately be able to begin chatting. If you don't see a channel which interests you, you can start your own and let people come to you.

Finding more information

IRC RFC 1459

Nicolas Pioch: *A Short IRC Primer* at http://www.irchelp.org/irchelp/ircprimer.html

Internet Relay Chat FAQ at http://www.kei.com/irc.html

IRC Central at http://www.connected-media.com/IRC/index.html

Neil Randall: 'Can we chat?' *PC Magazine Online* at http://www8.zdnet.com/pcmag/iu/toolkit/pctech-irc.htm

5 Providing Information

The information superhighway carries all sorts of traffic. There's a place for everything from the heavily-loaded lorry to the moped with a parcel strapped to the seat. There's also a choice of routes, and unlike some other superhighways, learner drivers are allowed on too.

Any type of information and any amount of it can be published on the Internet, whether it's a simple home page or a massive collection of institutional documents. While there are several ways of making information available, by far the most common and popular route is via the World Wide Web, which adds to the normal Internet benefit of easy and widespread distribution the advantage of attractive graphical and multimedia presentation capabilities. For simply making files available for downloading, an alternative route is via ftp. Public access to files in ftp archives is enabled through anonymous ftp.

Publishing via the WWW is likely to be the first choice for most Internet information providers. Simple Web publishing is easily achievable. Also the Web is currently the scene of phenomenal activity, not just in publishing, but also in software development. The possibilities for users and providers alike are constantly being increased and enriched by an exciting array of new tools and technologies. This chapter deals with some of those tools and technologies.

Topics to be covered include WWW authoring, Graphics in Web pages and finally interactive Web pages where we shall discuss Java, Javascript, CGI and Cookies.

5.1 WWW authoring

HTML (HyperText Markup Language) is the standard format for Web documents, and producing documents in HTML is currently the most basic requirement for providing information on the World Wide Web. There are many programs such as HTML editors, conversion programs and Web site development tools which can help. A brief descriptive list of selected WWW authoring tools (see Section 5.1.5) provides a starting point for seeing which tools are available. For further information, refer to other listings such as:

- Yahoo's list of clients `http://www.yahoo.com/Computers_and_Internet/Software/Internet/World_Wide_Web/HTML_Editors/`,
- the Web Consortium's list of WWW and HTML Tools `http://www.w3.org/pub/WWW/Tools/`,
- Carl Davis's HTML Editor Reviews `http://homepage.interaccess.com/~cdavis/edit_rev.html`.

5.1.1 HTML editors

HTML editing software spans the range of functionality from plain-text editors to packages which automatically generate HTML markup behind a WYSIWYG graphical interface. Some authors feel at home with raw HTML and choose to use a plain-text editor (such as BBEdit) thus exercising full control of the document. But for those who prefer not to concern themselves with HTML code, there are a number of WYSIWYG editors to choose from, such as Adobe PageMill or Netscape Composer. These allow the author to input text as though typing into a Web browser. Some programs such as HotDog Pro aim to give the control that code-based working provides but still allow easy monitoring of the appearance of the document using an inbuilt browser. Others such as HoTMetaL PRO allow the author to choose their mode of working, WYSIWIG, code-based, or an intermediate level where HTML tags can be seen. Flexible programs allow for easy switching between modes, and for editing in either mode. See Section 5.1.5 for more information.

5.1.2 Documents in other formats

Many Web documents start life as word-processing, spreadsheet, presentation or other files, and are then converted to HTML, either by specialist conversion utilities (such as RTFtoHTML) or with one of the more powerful HTML editors (such as HoTMetaL PRO) which enable the import of files in various common formats. Some commonly used word processors offer easy creation or conversion to HTML, for instance through a simple `Save as HTML` command. Microsoft Word 97 not only offers a painless conversion function, but provides for creation of documents in either Word format or HTML format as a standard function. With facilities such as these, the need for specialist conversion utilities is already diminishing for commonly used file formats. Meanwhile, developing technologies such as ActiveX and OLE are being used for viewing documents in their native format, obviating the need for conversion. As these techniques and standards advance, the need for HTML conversion may eventually become redundant.

To find references on the many conversion utilities available, see:

- NCSA's list of Converters to and from HTML together with archived messages of the HTML Converters discussion forum at http://union.ncsa.uiuc.edu/HyperNews/get/www/html/converters.html.
- the Web Consortium's list of HTML converters at http://www.w3.org/pub/WWW/Tools/Filters.html.

5.1.3 Web site development tools

With large collections of Web documents, there is a need for something more than HTML editors which focus on individual Web pages. Powerful all-in-one Web site development tools such as Microsoft Front Page provide the functionality both to edit individual pages and also view and manage whole sets of documents on a Web site. They may include features such as:

- easy, graphical HTML page creation,
- tools for designing the structure of a Web site,
- import of documents in other formats,
- tools for adding interactivity to pages,
- verification of links,
- graphics handling,
- global find and replace,
- database connectivity,
- simple upload to server.

5.1.4 Validating HTML

If Web authors wish to provide pages which are accessible to the widest possible audience, they should check that their HTML conforms with current standards. This process is known as **HTML validation**. Information on the current standard is available on the Web site of the World Wide Web Consortium, via http://www.w3.org/.

HTML editing programs commonly provide an HTML validation function, and may even enforce conformance to standards as the HTML is generated, for example HoTMetaL PRO. Alternatively documents can be run through an HTML checking program, either locally, or by using an online service such as:

- **HTMLValidation Service** http://www.hensa.ac.uk/html-val-svc/ On-line testing of HTML. Specify which HTML standard.
- **A Kinder Gentler HTML Validator** http://ugweb.cs.ualberta.ca/~gerald/validate/ Easy-to-use HTML document checking for compliance with HTML standards.
- **NetMechanic: Online Link Testing, HTML Validation** http://www.netmechanic.com/ Online testing for broken links, invalid HTML, and server response time.

5.1.5 WWW authoring tools

Adobe PageMill

Adobe PageMill (see Plate 6) is a WYSIWYG HTML editor that lets you build Web pages, manipulate images, and edit text with ease.

Features

- Imports files from other applications,
- toggles between source code and graphical view,
- support for tables, frames, Java applets,
- automatic upload via ftp,
- support for Netscape plug-ins,
- Adobe SiteMill(R) to help manage your Web pages,
- animations, sounds, templates and clip art to get you started.

Access Apple Mac (with Photoshop LE and Adobe SiteMill), Windows 95/NT (with Photoshop LE). For details, see Overview of Adobe PageMill at `http://www.adobe.com/prodindex/pagemill/overview.html`.

BBEdit

BBEdit is a plain-text HTML editor for the Macintosh providing tools that simplify and speed HTML coding.

Features

- Tool palette,
- drag and drop tools,
- form and table tools,
- syntax checking,
- search and replace.

Access Available from Bare Bones Software. Demonstration version is available free from the BBEdit Page at `http://www.barebones.com/bbedit.html`.

Claris Home Page

This is an HTML editor offering users of all levels an intuitive interface to the design, editing and publishing of Web pages.

Features

- Frames, tables, form elements,
- built-in libraries for storing images, text, HTML,
- spell checking,
- direct HTML editing,
- imagemap creation,
- support for Java applets and QuickTime movies,
- built-in upload software.

Access Available for Macintosh and Windows 95/NT. More information from Claris Home Page at `http://www.claris.com/products/claris/clarispage/clarispage.html`.

HotDog Pro

HotDog Pro is a code-based HTML editor with a host of menu options and toolbars for editing and management of documents. The interface can be customized according to personal preference.

Features

- In-built browser,
- support for wide range of HTML elements,
- dialogues for inserting images and links,
- support for style sheets, frames,
- access to ActiveX, JavaScript and Java routines,
- site view from the Resource Manager showing links and images,
- HTML syntax checking,
- multifile find and replace,
- publish function.

Access Versions for Windows 3.1/95/NT. The software is available for purchase from Sausage Software at `http://www.sausage.com/`. A free 15-day trial version can be downloaded from this site.

HoTMetaL PRO

This is a fully featured hybrid code-based/WYSIWYG HTML editor. The recent version offers a site management tool as part of the package.

Features

- Supports wide range of HTML tags,
- tags shown as icons in WYSIWYG interface, or hidden as required,
- automatic conversion from all common word-processing formats,
- built-in image editing and imagemap creation,
- easy editing of tables,
- strict HTML validation,
- link checking.

Access Versions for Windows 3.x/NT/95, Unix and Mac can be purchased from the SoftQuad site at `http://www.sq.com/`. A free trial version is available.

Microsoft Front Page

This tool is a complete Web site development tool including a WYSIWYG editor and project management tools, enabling authors to produce sophisticated Web pages without the need to *know* HTML. Bonus Pack includes

Image Composer, Personal Web Server, Web Publishing Wizard and Internet Explorer.

Features

- Graphical interface to creation of HTML, tables, frames, and so on,
- easy import of existing Web sites and content,
- wizard help,
- drag and drop components,
- graphical views of site structure and links,
- automatic verifying of links,
- database connectivitiy and querying,
- ActiveX and Java support,
- automated addition of advanced interactive functionality such as full-text searching.

Access Versions for Windows 95, Windows NT and Apple Mac. Available from Microsoft resellers. Online ordering is also possible – follow the links to `Shop` from Microsoft Front Page page at `http://www.microsoft.com/frontpage/`.

Microsoft Word Web Tools
This package includes a set of tools for browsing and authoring Web documents. Menu selection and use of ready-made tools and multimedia effects make for quick and efficient Web authoring.

Features

- WYSIWYG authoring,
- more than 80 common HTML tags supported,
- set of ready-made templates for different types of pages (easy start for beginners),
- wizard help,
- ready-made libraries of graphics, and so on.

Access Integrated Web authoring with Word 97. With previous versions of Word, the add-on Internet Assistant package needs to be installed. Word 97 is available from Microsoft resellers.

Netscape Composer
This is an easy-to-use WYSIWYG HTML editor. It comes as part of Netscape Communicator package, Netscape's integrated package for email, groupware, authoring and browsing.

Features

- HTML editing for common formatting tasks,
- supplemented by online Page Wizard and page templates on the Netscape Web site,

- WYSIWIG editing,
- spell checker,
- easy image import,
- one-button publishing.

Access Netscape Communicator is available for downloading from the Netscape Web site at `http://www.netscape.com/`. See the site for payment details. The package is available free for users in education and non-profit organizations. Prior to Communicator's release, Netscape's HTML editor was Netscape Gold.

5.2 Graphics in Web pages

5.2.1 Image formats

Common image formats in Web pages are:

- GIF (Graphics Interchange Format),
- JPEG (Joint Photographic Experts Group),
- PNG (Portable Network Graphics).

GIF and JPEG formats are supported by all graphical Web browsers. The GIF format is most suitable for line-art images such as icons, graphs and line-art logos. JPEG is better for photographic images. One major difference is in the number of colours supported. GIF supports up to 256 colours, while JPEG can use 16.7 million colours. PNG is a newer format, designed to overcome the deficiencies and restrictions inherent in the earlier formats. Native support for PNG is included with a number of browsers including Internet Explorer (4.0 and later versions).

See a reference to current information on browsers which support PNG in the Bibliography.

GIF

The Graphics Interchange Format is a common image format used in Web pages. It was originally developed by Compuserve. There are two versions of the GIF format: versions 87a and 89a. The format includes a number of useful features:

- **file compression** The GIF image format uses a built-in LZW compression algorithm, for which Unisys Corporation hold the patent. Commercial vendors, whose products use the GIF LZW compression, must license its use from UNISYS, but end-users do not need to pay to use GIFs.

- **transparency** Both GIF formats support transparency, but Version 89a also supports background transparency. This means that the background of an image can be made to appear the same colour as the background of the Web page, which is a standard technique.
- **interlacing** Interlacing allows for progressive enhancement of the image as it loads. Window blinds provide a rough analogy of interlacing versus the absence of it. An **interlaced GIF** is like gradually closing a finely slatted Venetian blind, in contrast to pulling down a Holland blind.
- **storage of multiple images within a single file** This feature provides the basis for a primitive form of animation which features prominently on many Web pages. This is the **animated GIF**. Animated GIFs are actually a compound image consisting of a set of separate images displayed at timed intervals, thus providing the effect of animation. The GIF89a format includes enhancements which make this possible.

  For information on how it's done, see *GIF89a-based Animation for the WWW* at `http://members.aol.com/royalef/gifanim.htm`.

See references to further information on GIF in the Bibliography.

JPEG

Joint Photographic Experts Group or JPEG is commonly used for graphics in Web pages and is a particularly effective compression method for natural, photographic-like true-colour images.

progressive JPEG A progressive JPEG is transmitted and displayed in a sequence of overlays, with each overlay becoming progressively higher in quality.

See references to further information on JPEG in the Bibliography.

PNG

The Portable Network Graphics format was designed to be a patent-free successor to the GIF format. Though not designed specifically for the Web, PNG offers particular benefits in this environment such as improved image compression (10% to 30% smaller than GIFs), two-dimensional interlacing and storage of text with an image making it possible for search engines to gather information and offer subject searching for images in a standard way.

For authors wishing to produce images in PNG format see the Web page on *Third Party Applications with PNG Support* at `http://www.wco.com/~png/pngapps.html`.

5.2.2 Efficient and effective images

There are many issues for the Web author to take into account in producing graphics. One of the most crucial for usability is that of **efficiency**. Can the user download the image within a reasonable time? In estimating download time, bear in mind that many users download Web pages at an average of 1k per second. For the Web author, there are various ways of reducing file size, and some Web authoring tools include helpful functions in this area, for instance encouraging authors to add height and width parameters to the IMAGE tag. Graphics packages too offer ways of minimizing file size, if the author is knowledgeable enough to recognize them. The Bandwidth Conservation Society at `http://www.infohiway.com/way/faster/` offers a lot of information on techniques for minimizing file size. See also *Conservation on the Web: Making Smaller GIFs* at `http://members.aol.com/royalef/conserva.htm`.

One issue which has considerable impact on the size of images is the number of colours used. Netscape uses a general purpose palette to render images. This palette consists of 216 distinct colours. To help ensure that Web graphics are rendered as intended, it is a good idea for authors to use this 216-colour palette as a starting point when creating images. Some Web graphics packages will allow you to specify the palette to use. You can find the Netscape Color Palette Map at `http://the-light.com/colclick.html`. Having started with this palette, it can then be reduced for individual images, depending on the number of colours used. The fewer the colours, the less data, the smaller the filesize, and the faster the download.

5.2.3 Animation and 3-D

Animation effects on the Web can be achieved with animated GIFs, Javascript, Java and by generating animation files in formats such as MPEG, AVI, QuickTime and Shockwave/Director. VRML is an open standard for 3-D multimedia and shared virtual worlds on the Internet.

Animation

For a basic introduction to multimedia on the WWW including animation, see the Web Developers' Virtual Library at `http://www.stars.com/Multimedia/`.

MPEG (Moving Picture Experts Group) is a widely used standard for digital compresssion of moving images. An extensive list of MPEG pointers and resources can be found at the MPEG.ORG Web site at `http://www.bok.net/~tristan/MPEG/MPEG-content.html`.

3-D

VRML (Virtual Reality Modelling Language) is a standard for the definition of three-dimensional environments used on the WWW. Simple VRML files can be created with a plain-text editor, or for more complex model building, modelling software will probably be required. VRML files are viewed with a VRML helper application or plug-in in conjunction with a Web browser. Examples of plug-ins are Cosmo Player or Sony's Community Place.

Information on development tools, browsers, plug-ins, and so on is available on the VRML Repository at `http://www.sdsc.edu/vrml/`. See additional references in the Bibliography.

5.2.4 Imagemaps

Imagemaps allow users to access different documents by clicking different areas in an image on a Web page. Imagemaps can be implemented on the server or on the client. The maps work by defining the active area of an image, including shape, size and destination in a text file, which is effectively the *map* data. This map is associated with an HTML file which includes the image. With server-side imagemaps, the map information is stored on the server. With client-side imagemaps, the map information can be specified in the same HTML file that contains the image. The browser parses the map, remembers the contents, and can respond to a click from the user and access the URL specified in the location. Client-side image maps have a number of advantages including faster access to documents referenced in the map. Tools such as MapEdit can be used to generate imagemaps.

See *Imagemap Authoring Guide and Tutorial Sites* at `http://www.cris.com/~automata/tutorial.shtml` for references to further information.

5.2.5 Graphics application software

Adobe Photoshop

Adobe Photoshop is a professional package for photo design and production with a rich array of functionality. It is the obvious choice for creation of high quality graphics for the Web.

Features

- Support for multiple layers in images,
- task automation and batch processing,
- professional photography tools,
- assortment of painting and drawing tools,
- sophisticated selection capability,
- multiple options in user interface,
- filters,
- transformations,
- multi-language support.

Access Mac, Windows, Unix. `http://www.adobe.com/prodindex/photoshop/`.

Paint Shop Pro for Windows
This is a shareware graphics editing, viewing and conversion package.

Features

- Supports over 30 image formats,
- numerous drawing and painting tools,
- dockable tool bars,
- enhanced selection options,
- built-in special effects filters,
- RGB colour separation.

Access Windows 95/NT. `http://www.jasc.com/pspdl.html`.

Graphic Workshop for Windows
Also shareware, this is a general multifunctional graphics package.

Features

- Converts between virtually all image formats,
- views graphics in any of the supported formats,
- displays a slide show of images,
- flips, scales and crops,
- applies sophisticated image filters to graphics, including soften, sharpen, emboss and edge detection,
- maintains an image database with keyword searching.

Access Windows 3.x/95/NT. `http://www.mindworkshop.com/alchemy/gww.html`.

GIF Construction Set for Windows
This is special-purpose software (shareware) for creating transparent, interlaced and animated GIF files for Web pages.

Features

- Easy interface to creating transparent GIF files,
- builds GIF files through Drag and Drop,
- supercompresses GIF files,
- creates animated LED signs,
- flips, rotates, scales and crops all or part of an animated GIF file.

Access Windows 3.x/95/NT. `http://www.mindworkshop.com/alchemy/gifcon.html`.

MapEdit
MapEdit is a graphical editor for World Wide Web imagemaps (clickable imagemaps).

Features

- Easy creation of client-side imagemaps,
- supports GIF, JPEG and PNG formats,
- will also create server-side maps for backwards compatibility with old browsers.

Access Windows 3.x/95/NT, Unix. `http://www.boutell.com/mapedit/`.

GifBuilder
This is a utility to create animated GIF files on the Macintosh.

Features

- Can collect PICT, GIF, TIFF or Photoshop images,
- can convert QuickTime movies, FilmStrip or PICS files,
- outputs GIF89a file with multiple images,
- Version 0.5 features frame icons in the Frames window,
- filters,
- transitions,
- animation cropping.

Access For Apple Mac. Available from `http://iawww.epfl.ch/Staff/Yves.Piguet/clip2gif-home/GifBuilder.html`.

5.3 Interactive Web pages

Interactivity in the World Wide Web is a broad concept covering techniques and technology that introduce dynamic behaviour into the Web.

The process by which a page is fetched on the Web is an inherently static procedure:

(1) A browser requests a document at a particular address (URL).
(2) The server at that site fetches the requested HTTP document (for example, a page in HTML, an image, a video) and transmits it back to the requester.
(3) The document is displayed by the browser.

In the variety of methods available for making the Web interactive each of these three stages can be enhanced or altered. Some, such as Java and Javascript, affect the display of the document by having the processing that provides the interactive behaviour performed by the browser. In contrast, the Common Gateway Interface extends the work done by the server when it fetches a requested HTTP document, and the use of cookies alters both the initial request step by the browser, as well as requiring extra work at the server to fulfil a request.

This section presents a selection of the many ways of producing interactivity. The topics covered are:

- **Java applets** Java byte-code pulled across the network and executed by the browser when the appropriate tag is encountered in an HTML page;
- **Javascript, JScript** programs embedded inside an HTML page are executed on-the-fly by the browser;
- **Common Gateway Interface (CGI)** a standard for fetching Web documents generated dynamically. It provides a gateway between a browser which displays HTTP pages statically and data which may be changing or calculated that is to be available on the World Wide Web. For example, CGI may be used to search for data that is stored in a database, or to capture a still image from a video camera that is recording a scene out the window. A well-known instance of the latter is the Cambridge Panorama at `http://www.orl.co.uk/cgi-bin/pangen/v=to/a=1`;
- **Cookies** small pieces of data created by servers and stored at the browser. When a browser includes a cookie in a request, the server will process the cookie (or possibly generate a new one if the browser didn't include one) in some manner which may affect the content that is returned to the client. Cookies are often used for site monitoring – keeping track of which pages are popular, or simply remembering where a particular visitor has been before.

5.3.1 Other interactive technologies

The **Document Object Model (DOM)** (see `http://www.w3.org/pub/WWW/MarkUp/DOM/`), also known as **Dynamic HTML** is a model for interactivity where the content, structure and style of an HTTP document can be dynamically altered by programs or scripts executing at the client's computer. The model is currently in the process of being defined by a working group of the World Wide Web Consortium.

Another topic relevant to interactivity in the WWW is distributed object technology. Software component models, such as **CORBA** and **DCOM** provide a framework within which distributed software objects can communicate with each other, regardless of location or platform. The consequence of these component models for the Web is that they offer a means to easily integrate software components in order to generate new applications or to extend old ones. For example, browsers, protocols or commercial applications, with the added benefits of all the sophisticated distributed systems services and techniques that are available within the model can be used collectively.

For more information see the documentation on existing products that use this technology: JavaBeans (`http://java.sun.com/products/jdk/1.1/docs/guide/beans/index.html`) and ActiveX (`http://www.microsoft.com/activeplatform/actx-gen/actxovw.asp`).

5.3.2 Java

Java (see Plate 7) is a programming language from Sun Microsystems designed to run in a secure manner on any platform without modification of the source code. These characteristics make it ideal for developing network applications – programs that you can pull over from a remote machine and execute on your own computer. The most common manifestation of Java on the Internet is in the form of applets (small Java programs) which can be executed by Java-enabled Web browsers. The applet program is dynamically loaded across the Internet when the Web browser encounters an applet tag in an HTML document, and is executed inside the browser. Java's built-in security mechanisms prevent inadvertent or malicious interference by the applet with any other part of the user's system.

Using

Java applets can be run by any Java-enabled browser, such as HotJava from Sun Microsystems, Netscape Navigator and Internet Explorer. When the browser encounters an `<APPLET>` tag in the HTML document it fetches the applet from the remote site and executes it on the local computer.

In order to write applets or stand-alone applications in Java, necessary components such as the core classes, a compiler and an interpreter, can be downloaded for free in the form of Sun's JDK from JavaSoft (at `http://www.javasoft.com/`), and there are also commercial products such as Symantec Cafe available (`http://www.symantec.com/`). There is even a tutorial for beginner programmers at `http://www.javasoft.com/docs/books/tutorial/index.html`.

Examples

Many examples of applets can be found at repositories such as The Java Repository or Gamelan (`http://java.wiwi.uni-frankfurt.de/` and `http://java.developer.com/` respectively).

Some interesting individual examples of applets include Ians Rubik Cube Page (`http://www.internexus.co.uk/rubik.htm`), and the Mars Pathfinder simulation applet at `http://mars.graham.com/wits/`.

Finding more information

The Java Centre `http://www.java.co.uk/` includes among other things details of training courses, tutorials and exhibitions being held in the UK. One of the largest repositories of Java applets and resources, organized by functionality, is Gamelan (see above). The JavaWorld magazine is an online magazine (`http://javaworld.com/`) aimed mostly at programmers which contains lots of technical information and discussion about Java.

5.3.3 JavaScript and JScript

Both JavaScript and JScript are scripting languages suitable for producing Internet applications. They are most commonly used for small programs that are embedded inside a page of HTML and executed on-the-fly by a browser that incorporates such functionality. JavaScript was developed at Netscape, while JScript is the equivalent language from Microsoft. Another example of a lightweight scripting language is Microsoft's VBScript, a subset of the Visual Basic language.

JavaScript and JScript can speed up interactive behaviour by avoiding the need to use the network to enable simple functionality. For example, verification of data entered in a form at a browser could be implemented by using some JavaScript inside the HTML of the form. Simple checks on the data entered by the user (such as the validity of a date) could be carried out at the client through the JavaScript program. This reduces server load and improves performance at the client side. In general, the use of an embedded scripting language permits a more event-driven page, where actions can occur in response to mouse clicks or text entry at the browser.

Using

To run a program written in any scripting language inside HTML, your browser must be able to interpret the particular language that is being used. Both Netscape and Internet Explorer browsers can execute JavaScript programs, while only Internet Explorer incorporates JScript.

Examples

Examples of JavaScript and JScript abound on the web. See JavaScript Place at `http://garnet.irrs.mi.cnr.it/DocComber/jsplace/`, or Stephan Koch's JavaScript page (`http://rummelplatz.uni-mannheim.de/~skoch/`) for JavaScript examples and a tutorial.

Finding more information

Netscape has a great deal of information on JavaScript, including an overview at `http://home.netscape.com/eng/mozilla/Gold/handbook/javascript/introd.html` and an authoring guide at `http://home.netscape.com/eng/mozilla/Gold/handbook/javascript/index.html`. JScript can be downloaded from Microsoft's home pages (`http://www.microsoft.com/jscript/`), and likewise VBScript from `http://www.microsoft.com/vbscript/`. Documentation is also available at these pages, including FAQs and sample programs.

5.3.4 Common Gateway Interface

The Common Gateway Interface (CGI) provides a route by which dynamically generated non-WWW information can be made available via the Web. CGI enhances the interactivity and functionality of the Web by providing a means for Web servers to relay commands to other programs and have the results delivered back to the user interactively, via the Web browser.

Using

The typical CGI scenario is as follows:

(1) The user clicks on a link in a Web page which represents the URL of a CGI script, for example keyword search request.
(2) The URL request is sent by the browser to the Web server.
(3) The Web server executes the CGI script, for example a database search for the keyword.
(4) The script sends back the output and terminates.
(5) A dynamically generated HTML page containing the output is displayed by the browser.

A document retrieved using CGI will be indistinguishable to the requesting browser from a normal static Web document (although possibly the content of the page may make its origins evident).

The use of CGI on a Web server is usually strictly controlled by the server manager because of the security risks inherent in allowing untrusted users to execute programs on the system. To create the actual scripts or programs that do the work, any programming language can be used. Popular choices are scripting languages such as Perl or Python, and compiled languages such as C and Visual Basic are also often used.

Collections of sample programs

- CGI Resource Index `http://www.cgi-resources.com/`,
- CGI Collection `http://www.selah.net/cgi.html`,
- Matt's Script Archive `http://www.worldwidemart.com/scripts/`.

Examples

Examples of CGI programs are widespread on the WWW; they include counters, forms, guestbooks, imagemaps and interfaces to database collections. Search engines (such as AltaVista, see Section 3.1.2) are a good illustration of using CGI to access a database, and examples of CGI-based guestbooks (see, for example, `http://www.worldwidemart.com/scripts/examples/guestbook.shtml`) abound.

Finding more information

The specification of CGI can be found at NCSA (`http://hoohoo.ncsa.uiuc.edu/cgi/`), along with a primer, a tutorial, an archive of CGI programs and other useful information. The W3 CGI page at `http://www.w3.org/pub/WWW/CGI/Overview.html` contains links to more documentation and discussion about CGI.

5.3.5 Cookies

Cookies are a way of saving information on behalf of the Web server at the browser's site. A cookie is a small amount of data that is sent by the server the first time a user accesses the site and stored by the browser on the user's computer. When making requests the browser checks whether a cookie has previously been saved for that site and if so, sends the cookie back to the server along with the request for the page.

The contents of a cookie can be anything the server wishes to 'remember'. It must have an expiration date and is limited in size. Some browsers, such as Netscape, allow cookies to be turned off by the user if desired. Cookies have been perceived as a security risk and possibly an invasion of privacy, however they are not executable programs and cannot corrupt the user's system or introduce viruses.

Cookies were initially introduced by Netscape, and have since been adopted by most other browsers as part of the HTTP protocol. A Request For Comments (RFC) is in preparation, meaning that cookies are being adopted as an Internet standard protocol.

Access

Cookies are not something to which you would normally require access. They are used by the browser and server to help personalize your Web usage. However, if you should want to see what information is being collected on your behalf, the file or files are located on the same computer as the browser you use, and possibly in the same directory, though their location can vary with different browsers. To look at them, run a search of the hard disk for `cookies` and view with a plain-text program such as Notepad.

Using

A WWW user may not be aware that cookies are being set by the sites he or she is visiting, although some browsers can warn the user before accepting a cookie, or even not allow the cookie to be set. (There are also programs such as PGPcookie.cutter which can be used to turn cookies off or to find out which cookies have been set.) Since the data is stored on the client computer, a user can always delete or corrupt the relevant files if they do not wish to keep the cookies.

Incorporating cookies at a Web server requires either some CGI programming or the use of JavaScript.

Examples

Common uses of cookies include tracking which pages are visited by a user at a particular site over multiple visits, storing information such as name and password, or, at a site consisting of a sequence of ordered pages such as a training course, to remember where the user reached on his or her last access. In the commercial context, cookies may be used to store information on items ordered, the usual analogy being the shopping trolley to which items are added at intervals, with a final tally being made by reference to cookies.

Finding more information

An excellent overview of Cookies is at Cookie Central (`http://www.cookiecentral.com/index.html`), and there is another at Andy's Netscape HTTP Cookie Information (`http://www.illuminatus.com/cookie.fcgi`). The Cookie specification (draft RFC) can be found at `http://portal.research.bell-labs.com/~dmk/cookie.html`. Cookies were first developed at Netscape, where there is also a specification (`http://home.netscape.com/newsref/std/cookie_spec.html`).

6 Security and Encryption

Reliable security is essential for the transmission of sensitive and commercial data on the Internet, whether it is between individuals, companies, employers and employees, vendors or purchasers. The use of the Internet for electronic commerce, electronic publishing, distributed private databases, teleworking, collaborative working, online education, virtual meetings, and so on holds exciting promise. But most of these uses rely on the security of electronic transactions for their widespread viability. Security on the Internet is now a big issue and much effort is being invested in developing a security infrastructure which addresses current needs and concerns.

In exchanges of data, there are a number of basic security requirements. Special measures designed to meet these requirements need to ensure the following:

- that we can be certain of where the data originates (authentication);
- that the data has not been tampered with in transmission (data integrity);
- that the data cannot be read by any unauthorized person (privacy).

Encryption is integral to meeting these needs and forms the basis of many of the new tools for security and privacy, such as PGP. This chapter looks at some of these tools, in particular ones that relate to user requirements, rather than those specific to the security concerns of Web site administrators or system managers. Two obvious areas of interest are ensuring the privacy of email, and maintaining the security of transactions via the WWW.

6.1 Encryption and authentication

Encryption is the process of using a key (cipher) to scramble readable text into unreadable **cyphertext**, that is, text that can only be read by someone with the cipher for decrypting it. Encryption on the Internet has many uses, from the secure transmission of credit card numbers via the WWW to protecting the privacy of personal email messages.

Similarly, authentication is the process of using a key or key pair to verify the integrity of a document and its origin.

6.1.1 Methods of encryption

Single key encryption (conventional cryptography) uses a single word or phrase as the key. The same key is used by the sender to encrypt and the receiver to decrypt. Sender and receiver initially need to have a secure way of passing the key from one to the other.

Examples include IDEA (International Data Encryption Algorithm), DES (Data Encryption Standard), RC2 and RC4 (used in international versions of software such as Netscape Navigator).

Public key encryption uses two types of key for secure encrypted communication: a public key, which may be freely given out to others, and a secret key, which is known only by you. Thus, for secure communication, a total of four keys are required:

- the *sender* has a public key and a secret key,
- the *receiver* also has his or her own public key and secret key.

Using public key encryption to send a message is a three-step process:

(1) Sender and receiver exchange their public keys (their secret keys are never given out and can only be accessed by the owner using a password).
(2) The sender uses the recipient's public key in encrypting a message for sending.
(3) The recipient's complementary secret key is used to decrypt the received message.

Note that once the message has been encrypted using the recipient's public key, even the sender will no longer be able to decrypt the resultant encrypted message.

An example of public key encryption is RSA, the original public key encryption system invented by Rivest, Shamir and Aldeman.

Both types of encryption are employed by PGP.

Keys

Cipher keys come in various sizes (measured in bits), generally the bigger the better, though public key ciphers usually need to be longer than single key ciphers to achieve the same level of security. 128-bit single key encryption provides a high level of security, while encryption with a 40-bit key may not necessarily withstand a concerted effort to break the code.

While single key encryption systems provide an efficient method of encryption, they present no foolproof way of securely exchanging keys. Public key encryption gets around this particular problem. Public keys are intended to be distributed openly, and collections of public keys are available on public key servers. Note that public key servers do not undertake to check the authenticity of keys stored in their databases.

Digital signatures

A digital signature, like a handwritten signature, proves that the document to which it is attached does originate from the signer and that it hasn't been modified. In other words, it offers **authentication**.

In the context of sending an email, a digital signature is produced by a computation involving the sender's private key and the message itself. It is then attached to the message for sending. When received, other computations using the sender's public key can be carried out to verify the authenticity of the message.

Digital certificates (digital IDs)

Digital certificates are used to verify the identity of each person in an electronic transaction. Certificates are issued by trusted third-party organizations (Certificate Authorities). Certificate Authorities verify the authenticity of certificate requests, in particular the connection between a person's public key and his or her identification. They will then provide a unique digitally signed certificate which can be used as proof of identity in electronic transactions.

Digital certificates may be used in a range of situations, for example as an indicator of identity for clients entering Web sites (they may replace passwords). They may map to a user's email address.

Currently, certificate authority services are offered by bodies such as VeriSign, BelSign, Certisign Certification Digital Ltda, amongst others.

6.1.2 Status of encryption

Despite its track record as an effective security tool, obstacles to the widespread and effective use of encryption remain. A number of national governments see it not as a useful technical measure, but as potentially providing a shield for criminal or subversive activities. Government's concern to be able to tap into all forms of communications has led to proposals for key recovery systems (**key escrow**). Such systems would use a trusted third-party with which copies of private encryption keys would be deposited. Keys could then be recovered for legal purposes such as criminal investigation, if necessary. The case of the Clipper Chip in the USA, is another example of a government wishing to preserve its right of access to communications between citizens. Such measures have provoked a considerable amount of protest because they are perceived to pose a threat to privacy and security for net users.

Another obstacle is the well-known ban on the export of high grade encryption systems by the US State Department. As a result of this ban, US-developed software products such as Netscape Navigator and Microsoft

Internet Explorer used outside the USA incorporate only lower level security (40-bit) encryption.

One of the success stories of encryption is PGP (Pretty Good Privacy), a software package for use with email, which provides a high level of protection of privacy and is widely used. PGP is discussed in Section 6.4.

6.2 Secure email

Plain email is not a secure medium. Messages can be read by people with authorized (or unauthorized) access to mail servers which handle the mail, unlikely though this might be. There are a few basic requirements for secure and private exchange of email:

- **privacy** nobody other than the intended recipient can read the message;
- **authentication** we can be certain that the message comes from the person from whom it appears to come;
- **integrity** we know that a message hasn't been tampered with in transmission.

Where privacy, authenticity and integrity of information sent is vital, users will look for ways of making their email secure. There are a number of tools and standards available for the secure and private exchange of email, though unfortunately they don't necessarily interoperate with each other. The most widely used is PGP while others include S/MIME and PEM/MOSS.

6.2.1 S/MIME

S/MIME, developed by RSA, is a standard for secure email which extends the MIME specification. It is a consortium effort to integrate security into MIME, backed by Microsoft, RSA and others. S/MIME was designed as a standard which would integrate into application software, giving interoperability irrespective of platform. It uses encryption to protect message privacy, digital signatures and digital certificates to authenticate senders, and a secure hashing function to detect message tampering. It boasts an easy-to-use interface in which encrypted messages are denoted by a lock, and those with digital signatures are shown with a pen icon. Products incorporating S/MIME include Netscape Messenger.

S/MIME cannot interoperate with MOSS or PGP.

6.2.2 PEM/MOSS

PEM (Privacy Enhanced Mail) is an older standard for secure email, encompassing encryption, authentication and certificate-based key management. PEM public key management is hierarchical: keys are verified at trusted

Certification Authorities. MIME Object Security Services (MOSS) supersedes PEM.

MOSS is not interoperable with PGP.

6.3 Security on the Web

With the onward rush of electronic commerce on the Internet, there is widespread concern, particularly in the commercial sector, about security on the WWW. Customers want to be reassured about the safety of entrusting their credit card numbers to a Web form. Companies would like to know that they can rely on the Web as a secure medium for business transactions. Software developers have taken note of the needs, and Microsoft and Netscape have incorporated cryptography software into their respective Web browsers to facilitate secure transactions and messaging.

6.3.1 SSL

SSL (Secure Sockets Layer), developed by Netscape, is a protocol for secure and reliable communications between Web clients and servers. It uses encryption to keep messages private, authenticates the server, and ensures that data sent between client and server is not tampered with. It is implemented on both server and client. Clients which implement it include Netscape Navigator, Secure Mosaic and Microsoft Internet Explorer, and it is available with servers from Netscape, Microsoft, IBM, Quarterdeck, OpenMarket and O'Reilly and Associates.

SSL offers protection of commercial transactions such as giving a credit card number. It uses a secure form (the URL begins with `https://` rather than `http://`). Another indicator of SSL at work is the security icon in the bottom-left corner of the Netscape Navigator window. If documents are not secure, the key is broken; secure documents show a whole unbroken key.

6.3.2 SET

SET, or Secure Electronic Transaction protocol, is an open standard for the processing of credit card transactions over the Internet created jointly by Netscape, Microsoft, Visa and Mastercard. It allows different vendors' software to interoperate with other vendors' software. SET requires special software on both client and server.

6.4 PGP

PGP (Pretty Good Privacy) (see Plate 8) is a widely deployed encryption and authentication program used mainly for electronic mail on the Internet. It employs a number of different encryption algorithms.

Access

PGP 5.0 is available from the PGP Web site at `http://www.pgp.com/`.

Freeware versions of PGP for non-commercial use are available from the MIT site at `http://web.mit.edu/network/pgp/`.

Note that because of US export restrictions on cryptography, access to PGP for users outside the USA and Canada is currently restricted. Moves to explore possibilities for the legal licensing of PGP in Europe are underway. Meanwhile the PGP International home page at `http://www.ifi.uio.no/~staalesc/PGP/` is undertaking a massive scanning operation of the source code manuals for the purposes of making the software available. Check the site for details of current availability.

A PGP Key Server can be accessed at `http://www.pgp.com/keyserver/pks-toplev.cgi`.

Coverage

Features of the latest version of PGP include:

- powerful encryption including public key encryption;
- use of digital signature to protect email from tampering and alteration;
- seamless integration with Eudora for both the Windows and Macintosh platforms, Claris Emailer for Macintosh, and Microsoft Exchange and Microsoft Outlook for Windows;
- application launch from within PGP to quickly view an encrypted file;
- key server integration – automatic post of public key to a public key server. Also searching the key server for others' public keys;
- multiplatform support – PGP supports both Windows 95/NT 4.0 and Macintosh;
- choice of encryption algorithm.

PGP may be used for email and also to encrypt and store files on a personal computer.

Using

The latest version of PGP hides the complexities of the various encryption processes behind an easy to use interface where operations are carried out at the click of a button. What is actually happening behind the scenes when a mail message is encrypted and signed is as follows:

(1) A one-way hash of the message is generated.
(2) The hash value is signed with the originator's signature.
(3) The message and the signature are concatenated.
(4) A random session key is created.
(5) The signed message is encrypted with the session key, using a private key algorithm.

(6) The session key is encrypted with the recipient's public key, using a public key algorithm.
(7) The encrypted message and the encrypted session key are bundled together for sending.

Finding more information

More information can be obtained from the PGP Web site at `http://www.pgp.com/`.

7 Miscellaneous Tools

Included in this chapter is a tool which doesn't fit neatly into other established chapters of the book, but which nevertheless should be covered. This is File Transfer Protocol.

7.1 FTP

FTP (File Transfer Protocol) is a facility for transferring files between host computers on the Internet. Basically, it is a protocol, that is, a set of communicating conventions used by the computers involved in the transaction.

Access

The ftp protocol is incorporated into many different programs such as ftp client software, WWW browsers, Web authoring programs and others which transfer files on the user's behalf. A login and password is required to establish an ftp connection to a remote computer.

Access to many public archives on the Internet is available through **anonymous ftp**. There are basically two routes for using anonymous ftp:

(1) **ftp connection using an ftp client** When prompted for a login, type in `anonymous`, then give your email address as the password.
(2) **ftp using a Web browser**.

Using

Two of the most common ways in which ftp is used are retrieving software from public archives and uploading Web documents to a Web server.

Retrieving files
The Web will commonly be the route by which most users arrive at software on public archives that they want to retrieve. As with other Web retrievals, it is just a matter of point and click. If, on the other hand, you have been given the specific location of a file in a public ftp archive, you can use your

Web browser's Open Location or Open Page function (from the File menu) to key in the URL. The URL of a file on an ftp server takes the form:

```
ftp://domain/path/filename
```

This tells the Web browser all it needs to know to retrieve the file.

While a Web browser is probably adequate for much of the file transferring you will need to do, dedicated ftp client software such as **WSFTP** for PC Windows, **Fetch** for Apple Mac, or the Unix **ftp** program (type `ftp <hostname>` at the Unix prompt) provides more flexibility and power. For instance such packages will normally allow you to retrieve multiple files in one transaction.

Uploading files to your own directory space

The function of uploading Web documents is commonly built into Web authoring programs. Ftp client software can also be used. As well as providing for transfer of multiple files, client software may also enable you to change filenames in your directory on the remote ftp server, to create directories, to view files, to list the contents of a directory and other functions. You can also use Netscape to upload files to your own directory. You can access the directory using a URL which includes your login name and takes the form:

```
ftp://username@domain/path
```

General aspects of using ftp

Whichever tool you use, ftp needs the exact details in order to do its work. It requires:

(1) the name of host computer (the domain name or IP address),
(2) the location of file (the path),
(3) the filename.

When an ftp connection is established using a client program, a username and password will be asked for. In the case of public archives, you will be able to use anonymous ftp. If it is a computer on which you have an account, you will need to supply your usual username and password. Once successfully logged on, you will then need to decide on the mode of transfer. There are two options:

(1) ASCII (plain text)
(2) binary.

You will need to specify binary transfer for word-processed files, database files, spreadsheets, graphics, compressed files, and so on. ASCII transfer is used for plain-text files such as HTML files, postscript and anything produced with a plain-text editor. If binary files are transferred in ASCII mode, the transfer may not be successful and you may have a corrupted file on arrival. However, some ftp client software may be smart enough to recognize from the filename extension which transfer mode is required and Web browsers certainly take care of such details for you.

Examples

Downloading a file from a public ftp archive with a Web browser

The file `wsftp32.zip` is located in the public directory `/pub/mirror/win95/wcarchive/alpha` on the ftp server `ftp.uni-magdeburg.de`. To ftp it using a Web browser, select from the browser's menu:

```
File
Open page
```

Into the dialogue window type:

```
ftp://ftp.uni-magdeburg.de/pub/mirror/win95/wcarchive/alpha/
wsftp32.zip
```

Depending on how its preferences have been set, the browser will save the file to your disk, unzip it for you, or ask you what you would like done with it. This is all that is necessary to ftp using a Web browser.

Using Netscape to upload files

You can use Netscape to upload files to your own filespace on a server. Suppose you have a username `xenon` on the ftp server `sun1.ucs.tam.org` and your directory is `/user/xenon`. From the Netscape File menu, you could select the Open Location/Open Page function and type in:

```
ftp://xenon@sun1.ucs.tam.org/user/xenon
```

You would then be prompted for your password, and when that has been accepted, be presented with a Web page listing the items in that directory. You could then transfer files into the directory by dragging and dropping their icons into the page. If you don't mind sending your password in the URL, alternatively you could do this in one step by using:

```
ftp://xenon:password@sun1.ucs.tam.org/user/xenon
```

Finding more information

Postel, J. and Reynolds, J. (1985): *File Transfer Protocol (FTP)*, RFC 959

Deutsch, P., Emtage, A. and Marine, A. (1994): *How to Use Anonymous FTP*, RFC 1635, FYI 24

A Networking Software

A.1 World Wide Web clients

A.1.1 Netscape Communicator and Navigator

Netscape Communicator is a suite of tools that includes the powerful all-purpose multiplatform Navigator browser for viewing HTML documents, with support for tables, frames and inline images, as well as a variety of audio and video formats (via LiveAudio and LiveVideo), plus VRML files (via Live3D). Additional third-party plug-ins provide for the viewing of more exotic file formats within the Web document. Netscape supports Java and JavaScript and provides a powerful tool for coordinating all of these additional components with LiveConnect. Still important is the older facility of forms and CGI which enables users to input data for processing by other applications. All of these tools considerably extend the functionality and interactivity of Web pages.

The suite also includes an email program and News reader as well as tools for collaboration (Cooltalk) and authoring HTML documents (Composer). There are facilities for filing useful URLs (bookmarks), caching retrieved files, specification of proxies, secure transactions (via SSL) and customizing the appearance and operation of the browser.

The Netscape Communicator suite and Netscape Navigator are available in a number of European languages including Danish, Dutch, English, French, German, Italian, Portuguese, Spanish and Swedish.

Access details

`http://home.netscape.com/comprod/`

Commercial use is for a fee with a year's subscription. Free to educational institutions, charitable non-profit organizations and public libraries. Download of prerelease (beta) software and also of finalized versions for a trial evaluation period is free.

Platform

Windows 95, Windows NT and Windows 3.x: on Windows 3.x, CoolTalk and LiveVideo require Video for Windows.

Apple Mac: LiveAudio and QuickTime supported on Mac 68K and Mac PowerPC, Live3D on PPC only, LiveVideo and CoolTalk not available for Mac.

Unix: some plug-ins are not available on the Unix version, for example, LiveAudio, Live3D, LiveVideo, QuickTime. CoolTalk helper application is available.

A.1.2 Microsoft Internet Explorer

This is a powerful multifunction browser for viewing HTML documents with integrated viewing of standard format image, video, audio (via ActiveMovie) and VRML files. As well as frames and tables, IE offers improved control over the layout and design of pages through the adoption of the Cascading Style Sheets standard. IE supports Java and the scripting languages JScript and VBscript, as well as plug-ins, and ActiveX (Windows 95 and NT only), a technology for bringing Windows-style applications to the Web. IE offers Mail and News capabilities plus tools for workgroup collaboration (NetMeeting). Internet Explorer provides for the caching of fetched pages, secure communication, authentication and the use of proxies. The appearance and operation of the browser can be customized to suit.

Access details

`http://www.microsoft.com/ie/`

Full installation includes mail and news clients, NetMeeting, ActiveMovie and ActiveX HTML layout control. Minimum recommended install is the browser plus mail and news.

Platform

Windows 95 and NT: versions for these platforms are generally in the lead with new developments.

Windows 3.x: development may lag behind versions for Windows 95 and NT.

Apple Mac: development may lag behind versions for Windows 95 and NT.

A.1.3 Lynx

Lynx is a fully featured plain-text World Wide Web browser for access from character-based terminals. Lynx displays HTML documents as plain text, providing support for most common HTML tags, including plain-text rendering of tables and frames. Its functions include support for forms, menu rendering of imagemaps, caching of pages, a history function and bookmarks. Further information is available at `http://lynx.browser.org/`.

Access details

Lynx software availability: `http://www.crl.com/~subir/lynx.html`.

Version for DOS and Win 32 (fdisk.com): `http://www.fdisk.com/doslynx/lynxport.htm`.

For public access via telnet to a Lynx client, see the list of sites at: `http://www.crl.com/~subir/lynx/public_lynx.html`.

Platform

Unix: VMS, DOS and Win 32.

A.1.4 CyberDog Internet

This browser is for the World Wide Web, with email and News capability as well as integrated viewing of movies, sounds and pictures, and Quicktime VR files. It includes a facility for filing notes on useful URLs and other references.

Cyberdog's use of OpenDoc component technology provides complete integration into the operating system and the potential for extension with other OpenDoc components.

The browser provides for a range of flexible uses including the creation of custom applications to access the Internet. Cyberdog supports Navigator plug-ins and Java with the Macintosh Runtime for Java.

Access details

`http://cyberdog.apple.com/`.

Platform

Apple Mac.

A.1.5 Mosaic

In its role as a pioneering graphical Web browser, Mosaic, from NCSA, was important in the Web's early rapid growth. Mosaic gives access to Web, gopher, ftp and News servers, and displays HTML, text, GIF, JPEG and XBM files. It provides support for tables, client-side imagemaps, a hotlist facility, history, email sending, and configuration of preferences for caching, use of proxies, helper applications and other functions. Some less common features are AutoSurf, a facility for the easy download of a number of documents linked to a specific HTML document, Kiosk Mode for limiting functionality or files available to users, a collaboration facility for real-time exchanges of messages, sharing of files and data with other Mosaic users, and support for Kodak PhotoCD files.

Access details

Free. Available from: `http://www.ncsa.uiuc.edu/SDG/Software/`. A number of commercial browsers based on NCSA Mosaic have been developed.

Platform

Current version is available for Windows 95, Windows NT and Windows 3.1x.

Further information on additional Web browsers

WWW FAQ at `http://www.boutell.com/faq/`

Software Tools for the World Wide Web at `http://www.ncl.ac.uk/wwwtools/report/index.html`

Glossary

ActiveX A technology developed by Microsoft. With an ActiveX-enabled browser (that is, Internet Explorer only) ActiveX controls can be downloaded as part of a Web document to add functionality to the browser (similar to Java applets). In particular ActiveX enables seamless viewing of Windows files of all types, for example spreadsheets, and in combination with other technologies such as Java and scripting languages, makes possible the development of complex Web applications. Currently it runs on 32-bit Windows platforms (Windows 95 and NT) only.

Aglet A Java object that can move from one host on the Internet to another. That is, an aglet that executes on one host can suddenly halt execution, dispatch to a remote host, and resume execution there. When the aglet moves, it takes along its program code as well as its state (data). A built-in security mechanism makes it safe for a computer to host untrusted aglets.

Avatar A graphical image of a user, such as used in graphical real-time Chat applications, or, a graphical personification of a computer or a computer process, intended to make the computing or network environment a more friendly place.

Caching Retrieved Web documents may be stored (cached) for a time so that they can be conveniently accessed if further requests are made for them. Caching of files considerably speeds up retrievals, whether it is handled by the browser itself, a local **proxy server**, or a regional caching server for a wider community. The issue of whether the most up-to-date copy of the file is retrieved is handled by the caching program which initially makes a brief check and compares the date of the file at its original location with that of the copy in the cache. If the date of the cached file is the same as the original, then the cached copy is used.

Web browsers normally maintain a cache of retrieved documents and this cache is used for retrievals where possible. In addition, the user may configure the browser to point to a caching server via the browser's options or preferences. File requests not able to be supplied from the browser cache would then be directed to the caching server. The caching server would supply the files from its cache if they were current, or pass on the request to the originating server if they were not.

Client–server A model of interaction between computers which is commonly used on the Internet. Users employ client software, such as a Web browser, to request information from servers. Servers, such as WWW servers, supply information in response to requests from clients. The client, which is normally installed on the user's computer, displays the information for the user. For instance, when a Web document is retrieved from a remote server, the client will interpret the HTML tags and display the document appropriately. Some aspects of how documents are delivered and displayed may be determined by the user through configuration of the client's settings, for instance size and colour of font, whether images are displayed, whether cookies are accepted.

In the client–server model, clients and servers have a special relationship derived from the common use of a well-defined set of communicating conventions (protocol). For example, Web browsers and servers use the WWW protocol, HTTP (HyperText Transfer Protocol). Web browsers generally can use other Internet protocols as well. In this way they can also retrieve information from ftp servers, gopher servers, and so on.

The client–server model of processing is one of the cornerstones of the Internet's success. It is an efficient system which distributes the processing load between client and server, and also gives the user some control over his or her own interface to Internet information.

Cookies A means for a Web server to induce a client to store information about itself which can subsequently be called up by the Web server when required. This might be information which users have supplied about themselves, their preferences or their requirements via forms input. The oft-cited example is the shopping list which might be added to from time to time. Cookies are currently implemented by Netscape and Internet Explorer.

More information can be obtained from `http://www.netscape.com/newsref/std/cookie_spec.html`.

Forms A defined area of an HTML document such as a window or box into which the user is able to input data in order to have it processed by another application, for instance to run a search on a database. The HTML standard provides support for forms in Web documents. The data keyed into the form is passed to a CGI (Common Gateway Interface) script which then passes it to the relevant application for processing. When the process is complete, the output is passed back, again using CGI, and the results presented to the user as some new HTML generated on the fly.

H.323 An ITU (International Telecommunications Union) standard for videoconferencing over local area networks and packet-switched networks generally. It is based on a recognized real-time standard and is commonly used with video over the Internet to ensure that users can communicate with each other, as long as they are using videoconferencing software which complies with the standard, for example Microsoft NetMeeting, Netscape Conference. The standard applies both to one-to-one and multiparty videoconferences.

HTML (HyperText Markup Language) The native language of the World Wide Web in which Web documents are normally written. HTML enables links to be specified, and the structure and formatting of Web documents to be defined. HTML documents are written in plain text, but with the addition of tags which describe or define the text they enclose. For example, a link is defined by the ANCHOR `<A>` tag placed around the hyperlinked text. It specifies the URL of the 'linked to' document, for example

```
<A HREF="http://www.terena.nl/gnrt/websearch/index.html">Web
Search Tools</A>
```

HTML is an evolving standard. Current work is focused on extending accessibility features, multimedia objects, scripting, style sheets, layout, forms, math and internationalization. See the World Wide Web Consortium site for current information.

HTTP (HyperText Transfer Protocol) The foundation protocol of the World Wide Web. It sets the rules for exchanges between browser and server. It provides for the transfer of hypertext and hypermedia, for recognition of file types, and other functions.

Hyperlink Example of hyperlink in an HTML document:

```
<A HREF="http://www.terena.nl/gnrt/websearch/index.html">Web
Search Tools</A>
```

When the HTML document is viewed with the Web browser, the tag information between angle brackets is not visible, but the words `Web Search Tools` are displayed in whatever format or colour is defined for links by the browser or the document's author (the browser default is often blue underlined text but HTML authors may specify any colour or style). When the user selects these words, the document `index.html` will be displayed, having been fetched from the Web server `www.terena.nl`, where it was found in the path `/gnrt/websearch`.

Imagemap Graphics containing active link areas, also known as **active maps**. Instead of the link being from a word or phrase in the document, it is embedded in a defined area of the imagemap. Clicking on that area fetches the referenced document. Imagemaps are often used to provide a graphical entry point to a Web site, though a text-based route through the site should always be given as an alternative.

ISDN (Integrated Services Digital Network) A system of digital telephone connections. It allows multiple digital channels to be operated simultaneously through a single, standard interface. The Basic Rate Interface (BRI) consists of two 64 kbps plus another lower rate channel to handle signalling. Primary Rate Interface (PRI) consists of 23 channels plus a signalling channel. ISDN is adequate for videoconferencing and other high bandwidth applications. The cost of an ISDN line is higher than a normal phone line, and special equipment is required.

JAVA Powerful, cross-platform programming language developed by Sun Microsystems. Java applets (small applications) may be incorporated into Web documents and can be executed securely by any Java-capable browser irrespective of whether it is running on a PC, an Apple Mac or a Unix workstation. Both Netscape Navigator and Internet Explorer are Java-capable. Java is being used in many ways which enhance the functionality and interactivity of Web pages.

JavaScript Scripting language (originally called LiveScript) developed by Netscape Communications for use with the Navigator browser. JavaScript code forms part of the HTML page and can be used, for example, to respond to user actions such as button clicks or to run processes locally or validate data. JScript is the Microsoft equivalent of Netscape's JavaScript for use with Microsoft's Internet Explorer.

MIME WWW's ability to recognize and handle files of different types is largely dependent on the use of the MIME (Multipurpose Internet Mail Extensions) standard. The standard provides for a system of registration of file types with information about the applications needed to process them. This information is incorporated into Web server and browser software, and enables the automatic recognition and display of registered file types.

Users can add other file types and associated processing instructions to their browser's configuration options if they wish.

Plug-Ins Browsers can display certain file types such as HTML and GIF as a standard part of their functioning. The display of other file types may be handled by additional software, either designed to work in conjunction with the browser for the display of a specific file type (a plug-in) or a stand-alone application which the browser can launch for viewing a file requiring that application (a helper application). With plug-ins there is closer integration with the functioning of the browser. Plug-ins are loaded when the browser is launched so can act instantly and non-intrusively when called upon, thus giving the browser the appearance of enhanced functionality. The idea of plug-ins was developed by Netscape but is also supported by Internet Explorer. Some plug-ins may be bundled with browser software, but many more from third-party developers are available for downloading.

Examples include Macromedia Shockwave which is used to display multimedia files from Macromedia Director, and Adobe Acrobat Reader which is used to display PDF files.

Further information on Netscape's plug-ins is available at `http://home.netscape.com/comprod/mirror/navcomponents_download.html`.

Proxy server Where a high level of security is required, a proxy Web server may be used to provide a gateway between a local area network and the Internet. The local network is protected by firewall software installed on the proxy server. This software enables the proxy server to keep the two worlds separate. All outward HTTP requests from the local network pass through the proxy server and similarly all information retrieved comes back in via the proxy server and is then passed back to the client. Using the options or preferences, Web browsers can be configured to point to the proxy server. Proxy servers will normally maintain a **cache** of retrieved documents.

URL (Uniform Resource Locator) A way of uniquely specifying the address of any document on the Internet. This is the lynchpin of WWW's embedded linking. The typical URL specifies the method used to access the resource (the protocol), the name of the host computer on which it is located and the path of the resource. For example

```
http://www.terena.nl/gnrt/websearch/index.html
```

The protocol specified in this example is http, the protocol of the World Wide Web. Other protocols can also by used within the WWW.

VRML (Virtual Reality Modelling Language) An Internet standard for the rendering of 3-D graphics. VRML files can be viewed with plug-ins such as Live3D.

WYSIWYG What You See Is What You Get. A graphical interface to a process which shows how the end-result will look as it is being produced. For example, a WYSIWYG HTML editor generates HTML markup but displays the document as if viewed with a Web browser.

Bibliography

General

Tanenbaum, Andrew S. (1996). *Computer Networks,* 3rd edn. Englewood Cliffs, NJ: Prentice Hall

Collaboration

Groupware on the Web: Classes, Species, and Instances
http://www.idbsu.edu/courses/mb581/workgrptech.html

LaLiberte, Daniel and Woolley, David: *Presentation Features of Text-based Conferencing Systems on the WWW*
http://www.december.com/cmc/mag/1997/may/lalib.html
Discusses structure and features of Web conferencing systems

Woolley, David R.: *Choosing Web Conferencing Software*
http://freenet.msp.mn.us/~drwool/webchoice.html
Article written for the 1996 International University Consortium Conference on WWW Course Development & Delivery

File formats

Bennett, Eric: *Cross-Platform Page*
http://www.mps.org/~ebennett/

Common Internet File Formats
http://www.matisse.net/files/formats.html
A list compiled by Eric Perlman and Ian Kallen, intended for Macintosh and PC Windows users

Compression FAQ (in 3 parts)
http://www.cs.ruu.nl/wais/html/na-dir/compression-faq/.html
Information on formats and tools for all platforms

Zhang, Allison: *Multimedia File Formats on The Internet*
http://ac.dal.ca/~dong/contents.html
Mainly for PC users

Intelligent agents

Agentsoft FAQ
http://www.agentsoft.com/faq.htm

IBM: The role of intelligent agents in the information infrastructure
http://activist.gpl.ibm.com:81/WhitePaper/ptc2.htm

O'Leary, Daniel: *Artificial Intelligence and Navigation on the Internet and Intranet*
http://ada.computer.org/pubs/expert/1996/opinion/x20008/x2008.htm

White, Jim: *Mobile Agents White Paper*
http://www.genmagic.com/agents/WhitePaper/whitepaper.html

Mailing lists

Aleks, Norm: *Mailing List Management Software FAQ*
ftp://ftp.uu.net/usenet/news.answers/mail/list-admin/software-faq

General User's Guide to LISTSERV, version 1.8c
http://www.lsoft.com/manuals/user/user.html

Kovacs, Diane, McCarty, Willard and Kovacs, Michael (1991): *How to Start and Manage . . . a List: A beginner's guide*
Send email to listserv@uhupvm1.uh.edu with the msg line get kovacs prv2n1 f=mail

Mailbase Documents for List Owners
http://www.mailbase.ac.uk/docs/owners-welcome.html

Milles: *Discussion Lists: Mailing List Manager Commands*
http://lawlib.slu.edu/training/mailser.htm
Email: Send message: GET MAILSER CMD NETTRAIN to LISTSERV@ubvm.cc.buffalo.edu

Netiquette

Dear Emily Postnews
http://www.clari.net/brad/emily.html

Rinaldi, Arlene: *The Net: User Guidelines and Etiquette*
http://www.fau.edu/rinaldi/net/index.htm

Quality of information

Clearinghouse: *Information: Ratings System*
http://www.lib.umich.edu/chouse/docs/ratings.html

How to Critically Analyze Information Sources
http://urisref.library.cornell.edu/skill26.htm

Information Quality – a collaborative gathering of thoughts and ideas
http://coombs.anu.edu.au/SpecialProj/QLTY/QltyDefinitions.html

Tillman, Hope: *Evaluating Quality on the Net*
http://www.tiac.net/users/hope/findqual.html

WWW authoring

A Compendium of HTML Elements
http://www.uni-siegen.de/help/html/compendium/

Baker, David W.: *WWW Authoring Information*
http://www.netspace.org/users/dwb/www-authoring.html

Case Western's Introduction to HTML
http://www.cwru.edu/help/introHTML/accolades.html

Driscoll, Harold: *HTML Validation Tools*
http://www.ccs.org/validate/validate.html

HTML Writers Guild's resource collection
http://www.hwg.org/resources/index.html
Links and describes many useful sites on all aspects of Web page and Web site development

Lynch & Horton: *Yale C/AIM Web Style Guide*
http://info.med.yale.edu/caim/manual/contents.html

NCSA Beginner's Guide to HTML
http://www.ncsa.uiuc.edu/General/Internet/WWW/HTMLPrimer.html

System P Table of Contents
http://globe2.gsfc.nasa.gov/SystemP/contents.html
Covers many aspects of WWW and HTML including lists of software

Tilton, Eric: *Composing Good HTML*
http://www.cs.cmu.edu/~tilt/cgh/

WDVL: *Introduction to HTML*
http://www.stars.com/Authoring/HTML/Primers/

Web Developer's Virtual Library
http://www.stars.com/

Webreference
http://www.webreference.com/

Yahoo's Links to Resources on HTML
`http://www.yahoo.com/Computers_and_Internet/Software/Data_Formats/HTML/`

Web graphics

Multimedia Web Publishing Tips
`http://www.metatools.com/webtips/webtip1.html`

Preparing Graphics for the Web
`http://www.servtech.com/public/dougg/graphics/`

Web Developer's Virtual Library Graphics page
`http://www.stars.com/Authoring/Graphics/`

Web PitStop Graphics page
`http://www.compware.demon.co.uk/pitstop/graphics.htm`

GIF

Frazier, Royal: *All about GIF89a*
`http://member.aol.com/royalef/gifabout.htm`

Frazier, Royal: *Making Animated GIFs* (part 1)
`http://member.aol.com/royalef/gifmake.htm`

GIF89a Specification
`http://www.w3.org/pub/WWW/Graphics/GIF/spec-gif89a.txt`

The Transparent/Interlaced GIF Resource Page
Adam Bernstein at `http://dragon.jpl.nasa.gov/~adam/transparent.html`

JPEG

JPEG FAQ
`http://www.faqs.org/faqs/jpeg-faq/`

Progressive JPEGs
`http://www.faqs.org/faqs/jpeg-faq/part1/index.html`

PNG

Portable Network Graphics
`http://www.wco.com/~png`

WWW and Online Browsers with PNG Support
`http://www.wco.com/~png/pngapbr.html`

Multimedia

Multimedia Authoring Web
http://www.mcli.dist.maricopa.edu/authoring/
Extensive listing of resources and tools

VRML

3-d Graphics for the World Wide Web: THE BASICS
http://www.stars.com/Authoring/Graphics/3d/
Tutorial on VRML

comp.lang.vrml FAQ
http://hiwaay.net/~crispen/vrml/faq.html
Answers basic questions and also points to current VRML standards

Index